AMISH ACRES®

Historic Farm, Restaurants, Theatre, Shops & Inns

Nappanee, Indiana

W9-AXW-192

Recipes

Visit our General Store online
for Oldfashioned shopping
a Newfangled way.

www.amishacres.com
800-800-4942

Introduction

Amish Acres in Nappanee, Indiana is the only Old Order Amish farmstead in America listed on The National Register of Historic Places. For over three of its thirteen decades the farm has been in a state of preservation for the purpose of interpreting Amish culture to an unfamiliar world. Among the traditions of these people who adhere to the patterns of life from 17th century European peasant culture, are retained the food habits of a time and place whose influence on American cuisine has been pervasive to the point of going unnoticed. This book of recipes illustrates through Amish Acres, along with friends and neighbors, the stalwart basics underlying adaptations that continue to grace the tables of church carry-ins, fund-raising events, frolics and family dinners.

Recipes that had originated in the German Alps, the Rhineland, or pastoral Alsace evolved often in new directions when the wives of the early German-speaking farmers began to deal with America's bounty. Of all the regional cooking styles, perhaps the most enduring and distinctive can be claimed by the Pennsylvania Dutch. They cherished the value of farm produce because in many cases their European enemies had destroyed their crops, cut down their orchards, and dug up their vines in dead of winter to drive them out. Rudyard Kipling was inspired to write that the Pennsylvania Dutch lived "as peaceful as Heaven might be if they farmed there."

Several years ago a young reporter from the British Broadcasting Company (BBC) came to Amish Acres seeking authentic, therefore quaint, recipes from the Amish who remain a curiosity in Europe today. In a recorded interview with Ruth Miller, Amish Acres' cook, the eager reporter thrust a microphone her way and asked in a quaint, to us, British accent, "Ruth, tell me some of your unique recipes." Ruth looked perplexed by the question. Finally, under a wrinkled brow, she said, "We have meat, potatoes, vegetables and fruit." The microphone clicked off as the reporter's exuberance turned to near despair. She was a long way from home!

Ruth had elegantly illustrated the simplicity of Amish attitudes toward food and its preparation. For the Amish it is sustenance for the body and mind, provided by Nature, already in a perfect state. What follows in this collection of recipes is, to many Amish, superfluous and fancy; however, the underlying reverence for Nature's gifts shines through our shared background and traditions, with each recipe, offered with respect and love.

This collection includes all of the recipes for our famous Threshers Dinner. This menu of recipes has been served since the family style restaurant opened in 1970. Nearly five million Threshers Dinners have been served in the barn restaurant over that period.

In a similar pattern of tradition, the Broadway musical about the Amish, *Plain and Fancy*, has been on Amish Acres stage since 1986. Celebrated in this love story is a cultural declaration - a nod to the bounty of the soil. In the rousing anthem, "Plenty of Pennsylvania," the Yoder family, in alphabetic order, pays homage: "Asparagus, broccoli, cauliflower, dandelion greens, and escarole, fennel, grapes, honeydew melon, and iceberg lettuce for the salad bowl, juniper, kale, lovely lentils, mushrooms, nutmeg, okra, peas, quinces, rutabaga, squash, tomatoes, oonions - sweet like strawberries, vinegar, also watermelon, xplant planted all in rows, yams and zpinach, zourkraut, no, zucchini."

Amish continue to make their kitchens the biggest rooms in their farmhouses, to serve as centers of food preservation. Centuries-old techniques for preserving vegetables and fruits are still practiced with each season's harvest. Their use of spices and herbs, as harmonious additives rather than as seasoning to shock the palate, are unlike any other cuisine. As the world's tables become more varied and regional dishes lose their flavor, the basics will always be rooted deeply in the soil of the Germanic farm families who bravely made America their home.

Since 1996 repertory musical theatre joined *Plain and Fancy* and Friday night Theme Buffets have accompanied each show. We have collected these recipes by show and given you the spice of time and place from the Barn Loft Grill.

In September of 2000, 471 direct descendants of Manasses T. Kuhns, the last Amish owner of the farm, gathered in family reunion. Many of the great great grandchildren were visiting their ancestral homestead for the first time. The Kuhns family brought well over one hundred of the recipes in this collection to the reunion.

Appetizers
& Drinks

Appetizer Meatballs
Mrs. Freeman Yoder, great-granddaughter of M.T. Kuhns

2 lbs ground beef
2 c milk
1/2 tsp pepper
1/2 tsp garlic powder
2 eggs

1 lb ground pork
2 c quick oatmeal
2 tsp chili powder
2 to 3 tsp salt
1/2 c chopped onions

Sauce:
2 c catsup
1 tsp liquid smoke
1/2 c chopped onions

1 1/2 c brown sugar
1/2 tsp garlic powder

Mix all meatball ingredients together. Shape into small balls.
Place in a baking pan in a single layer. Combine sauce ingredients
& pour over meatballs. Bake at 350 degrees for 1 hour.

California Onion Slim Dip
Susan Nunemaker

2 c cottage cheese (small curds)
1 envelope dry onion soup mix

1/4 c skim milk

Place skim milk & cottage cheese in blender. Blend on high speed
until smooth & creamy about 4 minutes. Stir in soup mix, cover
& refrigerate at least 1 hour. Makes 2 cups.

Cheese Ball
Greg and Marsolie Kuhns, great-grandson of M.T. Kuhns

2 - 8 oz cream cheese
A little garlic powder
A little Lawry's Salt
1/2 to 3/4 c shredded cheese

1 small jar smoked bacon
2 tsp onion
1 pkg dried beef, chopped
2 tsp Worcestershire sauce

Mix all together. I like to make mine a couple of days before
& let set covered in the fridge to help "blend" the flavors.

Cheese Dip for Chips
Frieda Miller

1 lb hamburger (browned)   2 lb Velveeta cheese
1 can tomatoes and green chilies   1 can mushroom soup

Put in casserole and heat till cheese is melted.
Can use a crockpot also.

Chip or Vegetable Dip
Laura Slabaugh/Frieda Miller

2 c mayonnaise   1 1/2 c sour cream
1/2 tsp onion salt   1/2 tsp garlic salt
1 1/2 tsp dill weed   1 1/2 tsp parsley flakes
1 tsp accent

Mix well and refrigerate.

Church Spread
Amish Acres Kitchen

16 oz peanut butter   1 1/2 c marshmallow cream
2 c karo syrup   1/4 c hot water

Mix all ingredients together until creamy.
Use as dip for vegetables.

Deviled Eggs
Greg and Marsolie Kuhns, great-grandson of M.T. Kuhns

12 hard cooked eggs cut in half - yolk removed
1 1/2 tsp dill relish   3/4 to 1 c real mayonnaise
3 tsp diced onions   1 1/2 tsp horseradish sauce
Salt & pepper to taste

Mash yolks with a fork. Add the other ingredients
& mix well. Stuff egg whites with yolk mixture.

Egg Rolls
Ruth Ann Miller

3 lb ground pork
1 head cabbage, chopped
Salt and pepper to taste
2 large cans bean sprouts
1/2 c soy sauce

2 lb fresh mushrooms
1 large onion, chopped
3 cans bamboo shoots
Garlic powder, to taste

Sweet & Sour Sauce:
2 Tbls ketchup
2 Tbls vinegar
2/3 c water

4 Tbls sugar
1 1/2 Tbls cornstarch

Brown pork in a large skillet, drain excess grease. Add cabbage, mushrooms, bamboo, sprouts, onions and seasonings. Heat just until cabbage gets limp. Drain mixture very well in colander. Heat Crisco oil for frying. Wrap vegetable mixture in egg roll skins purchased at grocery. Roll up and seal flap with a bit of water. Fry until golden. Mix ingredients for sauce and use on egg rolls.

Fruit Dip
Anna Marie Schmucker

2 - 8 oz cream cheese
3/4 c powdered sugar

1 - 16 oz Cool Whip
Pineapple juice

Mix together above ingredients. Add pineapple juice for right thickening. Chill. Serve with sliced oranges, bananas, grapes and apples.

Hot Chipped Beef Dip
Ruth Ann Miller

2 - 8 oz cream cheese, softened
2 Tbsp milk
1/4 c minced onion
   or 3/4 c chopped onion
2 - 3 oz packages chipped dried beef

1 c sour cream
1 Tbsp Worcestershire sauce

1/4 c chopped green pepper

Mix and bake at 350 for 30 minutes. Serve hot with crackers or melba toast.

Ham Tortilla Rollup
Nancy Hershberger

1 pkg 12 inch flour tortilla shells	2 - 8 oz cream cheese
1/2 c sour cream	8 oz shaved cooked ham
2 Tbsp green onion	1/4 c black olives (chopped)

Combine cream cheese, sour cream, onions and black olives. Spread mixture on a tortilla shell. Arrange ham over cheese mixture. Tightly roll up tortilla and wrap in plastic wrap. Refrigerate 3 hours or overnight. To serve cut in 3/4 inch slices.

Mexican Cinnamon-Sugar Chips & Fruit Salsa
Andrea Stahly

Chips

6 Tbsp sugar	1/2 tsp cinnamon
1 Tbsp light corn syrup	6 flour tortillas

Salsa

1 papaya (peeled, chopped, diced)	1 pear (peeled, chopped, diced)
6 strawberries	1 or 2 Tbsp sugar
1 banana diced	1 orange diced
2 Tbsp lime juice	

Dipping Sauce

2 tsp sugar	1/2 c whipped cream

Heat oven to 400 degrees. Mix sugar and cinnamon. Brush one side of tortilla with syrup and sprinkle with sugar mix. Cut tortillas into 6 wedges. Place on a cookie sheet; bake 10 minutes. While it's baking mix all the salsa ingredients into a bowl. Stir sugar into whip cream. Serve with salsa & whip cream.

Hot Crab Spread
Susie Pletcher

8 oz cream cheese
1 - 6 1/2 oz can crab
1/2 tsp cream style horseradish
Dash of pepper

1 Tbsp milk
2 tsp chopped onion
1/4 tsp salt
1/3 c almond slices

Combine and blend milk and cream cheese. Blend in rest of ingredients in blender, except almonds and spoon in oven safe dish. Sprinkle with almonds and bake at 365 degrees for 15 min. Left overs can be frozen.

Party Mix
Amish Acres Kitchen

1/2 c butter
3 Tbsp Worcestershire salt
5 c Rice Chex
2 c salted nuts

1 Tbsp seasoned salt
5 c Corn Chex
5 c Wheat Chex
2 c pretzel sticks

Preheat oven to 250. Melt butter in 4 inch pan. Add seasoned salt, Worcestershire sauce. Gradually add cereal, nuts and pretzels mixing until evenly coated. Bake on paper covered cookie sheet stirring every 10 minutes for 30 to 45 minutes. Store in airtight container.

Pickled Eggs
Theme Buffet: Fiddler on the Roof - Chef Brenda Ritter

1 1/2 dozen eggs
1 3/4 c cider vinegar
3 Tbsp sugar
1/4 tsp garlic salt
1/4 tsp dill seed
8 oz beet juice for color

1 medium onion sliced
3/4 c water
1/2 tsp salt
1 whole clove
5 or 6 peppercorns

Put eggs in cold water and bring to a boil and cover. Turn off heat and leave in water for 20 minutes. Cool and shell eggs. Put the rest of ingredients together in a small pan. Bring to a boil and simmer 5 minutes. Pour in jar over eggs.

Polish Spread
Bertha Hershberger

1 lb sausage (mild - hot)   1 lb hamburger
1 tsp oregano   1 tsp garlic powder
1 Tbsp Worcestershire Sauce   1 lb Velveeta cheese

Brown meat and drain off grease. Add oregano, garlic powder and
Worcestershire sauce. Add Velveeta cheese. Spread on party size rye
bread. Bake 10 to 12 minutes at 350.

Ritz Bits
Michan Eby

14 oz pkg Ritz bits   1 tsp dill weed
1 pkg dry Hidden Valley dressing   1/2 c vegetable oil

Mix the dressing, dill weed & oil together. Stir in with crackers.
Bake at 350 for 15 minutes in a shallow pan (watch closely).

Roasted Eggplant Dip
Ruth Ann Miller

1 eggplant   1 tsp chopped garlic
2 Tbsp capers   1/2 c mayonnaise
1 tsp lemon juice   1 tsp chopped shallots
1/2 tsp pepper   3 Tbsp dry sherry

Roast eggplant, peel and mash in a medium size bowl.
Add all listed ingredients, mix well, and chill.

Sugar Glazed Grapes
Theme Buffet: Man of La Mancha - Chef Brenda Ritter

1 c sugar   1/2 c water   Grapes

Boil sugar and water together for 5 min. Let cool. Dip bunches of
grapes in mixture, drain off, sprinkle grapes with coarse sugar.

Sweet and Sour Sauce
Ruth Ann Miller

2 Tbsp ketchup
2 Tbsp vinegar
2/3 c water

4 Tbsp sugar
1 1/2 Tbsp cornstarch

Mix and use on egg rolls

Tortilla Pinwheels
Jenni Pletcher-Wysong

8 oz sour cream
1 (4oz) can diced green chiles
1 c grated cheddar cheese
Garlic powder to taste
5 flour tortillas

1 (8oz) pkg soft cream cheese
1 (4oz) can black olives
1/2 c chopped green onion
Seasoning salt to taste

Mix all of the ingrediants, except tortillas, together. Divide the filling and spread evenly over the tortillas. Roll. Cover tightly with the plastic wrap, twisting ends. Refridgerate for several hours. Unwrap and cut into 1/2 to 3/4 inch slices; serve with salsa.

Traditional Swedish Meatballs
Andrea Stahly

1 lb ground beef
1/2 c bread crumbs
1/4 c diced onion
1/2 tsp pepper
oil

1 lb ground pork
1/2 c sweet cream
1 tsp salt
Pinch of nutmeg

Place beef, pork, bread crumbs and sweet cream in a mixing bowl. Let rest for a few minutes. Add remaining ingredients except oil and shape into balls. Heat oil and brown meatballs completely. Serve over buttered noodles.

Vegetable Meatballs
Mary Rader

1 lb ground beef	4 Tbsp ground celery
4 Tbsp grated ground carrots	1 tsp minced onion
1/4 c dry bread crumbs	2 eggs
1 1/2 tsp salt	1 c tomato juice

Mix all ingredients together except tomato juice. Shape into balls and place in buttered baking dish. Pour on the tomato juice and bake until cooked throughout. Serve plain or with tomato sauce. The balls are more attractive if they are browned slightly in butter before being placed in the baking dish.

Vegetable Pizza
Mary K. Bontrager, great-granddaughter of M.T. Kuhns

3 c flour	3/4 tsp salt
6 tsp baking powder	3/4 tsp cream of tartar
1/3 c sugar	3/4 c butter or lard
1 c milk	2 - 8 oz cream cheese (softened)
3/4 c mayonnaise	

2 Tbsp sour cream & onion powder
    or 1 pkg. Hidden Valley Ranch Mix
Any fresh vegetable of your choice.
    Broccoli, Cauliflower, Peppers, Onions, Bacon Bits or Meat Chips.

Shredded cheese	Diced tomatoes

Sift dry ingredients; cut in butter or lard. Add milk & stir with a fork until dough is moistened. (Do not overbeat) Spread in a greased pan (17x12) & bake at 450 degrees for 10 to 12 minutes.

Mix cream cheese, mayonnaise, & Ranch Mix. Spread on top of baked crust. Top with any variety vegetables. Then top with cheese & garnish with tomatoes.

Watermelon Rind Pickles
Jean Bolyard

7lb thick watermelon rind
1 qt cold water
7 c sugar
2 cinnamon sticks

1/4 c pickling salt
1 tsp alum (opt.)
2 c white vinegar
12 cloves in a spice bag

Trim pink flesh and green from melon rind so you have white pulp. Cut pulp into 1 inch cubes. Dissolve salt in cold water and soak melon-rind cubes overnight. Make more brine as needed to keep rind covered. Combine sugar, vinegar, cinnamon, and cloves in a saucepan. Bring to a boil and pour over rind. Cover and let stand over night. In morning, sterilize canning jars and lids according to manufacturer's directions. Drain off syrup into saucepan. Pack the rind into sterilized canning jar. Bring syrup to a boil and pour over rind in jars; leaving 1/2" head space. Seal with sterilized lids according to the manufacturer's directions. Process in boiling water for 10 minutes.

Berry Pineapple Slush
Andrea Stahly

1 - 20 oz can pineapple chunks juice, drained
2 c fresh/frozen unsweetened strawberries or raspberries
1 c orange juice   2 Tbsp sugar
1/4 c lemon juice from concentrate
1 liter bottle of ginger ale

In a blender mix first 5 ingredients. Cover and blend until smooth. Strain and discard seeds. Transfer to a 2 qt baking dish. Cover and freeze 24 hours.

To serve: Let stand at room temp for 20 to 30 minutes. With spoon, scrape surface and put slush into glasses. Add ginger ale and stir to mix.

Blackberry Fizz
Andrea Stahly

3 qts fresh or frozen blackberries
3 c sugar
1 Tbsp whole allspice
Lemon-lime or white soda

3 c water
1 Tbsp whole cloves
2 cinnamon sticks, broken into 4"

Crush blackberries in a large kettle. Add water and bring to a boil. Reduce heat to medium and cook for 10 minutes. Strain through a jelly bag. Reserve the juice and discard the pulp. Add water to juice if necessary to equal 2 qts; pour into large kettle. Slowly stir in sugar until dissolved. Place spices in cheesecloth bag; add to juice for 30 minutes; simmer uncovered. Bring to a boil, remove the spice bag and discard. Pour into hot jars leaving 1/4 inch headspace. Adjust caps. Process for 15 minutes in a boiling water bath. To serve: Mix about 1/3 concentrate to 2/3 soda.

Cappuccino
Anna Marie Schmucker

3 - 8 oz french vanilla creamers
1 c instant coffee (Maxwell House preferred)
1 c hot chocolate mix

3/4 c regular creamer
1 1/2 c powdered sugar

Mix together. Use 1/4 cup mix for one cup of cappuccino. Add hot water.

Cappuccino Mix
Bertha Hershberger

1 c coffee creamer
1 c instant chocolate drink mix
1 tsp cinnamon

1 c instant coffee
1/2 c sugar
1/4 tsp nutmeg

Mix all ingredients and store in air-tight container. Use 3 Tbsp mix to 6 oz boiling water.

Champagne Punch
Amish Acres Kitchen

1 - 12 oz can frozen orange juice concentrate
1 - 12 oz can frozen lemonade concentrate
6 c cold water
1 - 46 oz can unsweetened pineapple juice
2 bottles of extra dry champagne or 1 - 2 liter of ginger ale

Mix orange juice, lemonade, water, sugar, and pineapple juice together and freeze. When ready to serve punch use a long handled spoon to cut up the punch and then use an old-fashion potato masher. Mash the punch up until it looks like mush.
Add champagne or ginger ale.

Christmas Punch
Laura Slabaugh

4 pkgs lemon lime Kool-aid   3 qts water
3 c sugar   1 - 64 oz pineapple juice
2 sm or 1 large frozen orange juice (add water according to directions)
Lime sherbet

Put sherbet in punch bowl.
Add punch and a 2 liter of 7Up or Ginger ale

Fishmonger's Punch
Susie Kuhns, great-granddaughter of M.T. Kuhns

1 qt ginger ale   1 qt pineapple juice
1- 16 oz bottle grape juice   1 qt orange juice
1 qt lemonade (made from concentrate)

Combine all ingredients in a punch bowl & mix well. Add a large block of ice or several trays of ice cubes. Servings: 48 cups.

Fruit Slush
Mary Edna Kuhns, great-granddaughter of M.T. Kuhns

1 - 12 oz can frozen orange juice
1 qt canned peaches
1 c sugar (more or less to taste)

20 oz crushed pineapple
6 sliced bananas

Mix orange juice with 1 can water. Add pineapple and peaches with juices and enough water to make 3 cups of liquid. Add bananas and sugar, mix well and freeze

Green Punch
Ruth Ann Miller

1 - 6 oz lime Jell-O
2 qts boiling water
1 qt cold water

2 c sugar
1 - 46 oz pineapple juice

Mix boiling water and Jell-O, add rest of ingredients. Freeze. Remove from freezer 1/2 hour before serving. Add 7Up or Ginger ale. Should be slushy when serving.

Hot Buttered Rum
Bertha Hershberger

2 1/2 tsp brown sugar
3 oz rum
1 Tbsp butter

1 cinnamon stick
1 c hot milk

Sprinkle with nutmeg and add a dip of cool whip.

Hot Wassail Drink
Amish Acres Kitchen

18 c cider
3/4 tsp nutmeg
7 1/2 c unsweetened pineapple juice

3 sticks cinnamon
3/4 tsp honey
9 Tbsp lemon juice

Heat cider and sticks, add remaining ingredients. Stir and simmer slowly. Add whole orange studded with cloves.

Orange Jeffius
Jeff Stillson

1/2 c milk
1/4 c sugar
4 oz frozen orange juice

1/2 c water
1/2 tsp vanilla
6 ice cubes

Blend 45 seconds. Enjoy!

Party Punch
Jacob and Loretta Kuhns, great-grandson of M.T. Kuhns

7 c pineapple juice
3 c vanilla ice cream

1 pint sherbet
3 c chilled ginger ale

Mix in punch bowl. Serves 24 people.

Punch
Mrs. Steven Miller, great-grandchild of M.T. Kuhns

3 - 3 oz boxes strawberry Jell-O
6 c sugar

2 pkg cherry Kool-aid
8 c boiling water

Combine above ingredients in large container, stir until dissolved.
Add one large can unsweetened pineapple juice, one 6 oz.
Real lemon juice and one gallon water. Freeze.
When ready to serve add Sprite.

Punch
Ruth Ann Miller

1 - 6 oz pkg Jell-O
2 qt boiling water
1 qt cold water

2 c sugar
1 - 46 oz can pineapple juice

Freeze, stirring occasionally
Should be slushy, Serve with 7Up or Sprite.

Rhubarb Juice
Mrs. Arlin Hershberger, great-great grandchild of M.T. Kuhns

2 quarts rhubarb, cut up
2 1/4 c sugar
2 Tbsp yellow or 1 pkg. strawberry Kool Aid
1/2 c real lemon

Water
2 c pineapple juice

7Up

Cover rhubarb with water & boil 10 minutes. Put in colander & let drip 1 hr or more. Take 2 quarts juice, melt sugar in 2 cups hot water, add everything else but 7Up. Put in jars & cold pack for 15 minutes. Add 7Up when ready to use. 1 quart juice to 12 oz. 7Up.

Sherbet Punch
Rhoda Hershberger

1 gal cranberry juice cocktail
1 gal raspberry sherbet

3 - 2 liter ginger ales

Combine juice and ginger ale, add softened sherbet and stir.

Tangy Tomato Juice
Theme Buffet: **Big River -** *Chef Brenda Ritter*

1 qt tomato juice
2 Tbsp Worcestershire sauce

2 tsp Tabasco Sauce
2 tsp pepper

Blend together. Refrigerate.
Until smooth. Add milk if too thick.

Breads
& Rolls

Angel Biscuits
Mrs. Joseph Hostetler, Jr.

2 pkgs dry yeast (1/4 oz each)
2 c warm buttermilk
1/3 c sugar
1 Tbsp salt
1 c shortening

1/4 c warm water
5 c flour
1 Tbsp baking powder
1 tsp baking soda

Dissolve yeast in warm water. Let stand 5 minutes. Stir in buttermilk: set aside. In a large mixing bowl, combine flour, sugar, baking powder, soda, & salt. Cut in shortening until mixture resembles coarse meal. Stir in yeast/buttermilk mixture; mix well. Knead 3 to 4 times. Roll to a 1/2 inch thickness. Cut with biscuit cutter. Place on a lightly greased baking sheet. Cover & let rise in a warm place 1 1/2 hours. Bake at 350 degrees for 8 to10 minutes. Brush tops with butter.

Apple Bread
Nancy Hamman

3 c apples, chopped
1/2 c brown sugar
1 tsp baking soda
1 c uncooked oats
1 tsp cinnamon
2 eggs
1/2 c brown sugar

1/2 c water
2 c flour
1 tsp baking powder
1/2 tsp allspice
1 tsp salt
1/4 c oleo melted or oil

Combine apples, water and brown sugar and cook on stove top 5 minutes. Remove from heat and cool. Add remainder of ingredients. Mix all in order and bake at 350 for 40 minutes. Can use loaf or angel food cake pan.

Austrian Beer Bread
Theme Buffet: The Sound of Music - Chef Brenda Ritter

12 c flour
3 Tbsp sugar
4 - 12 oz beers

1/2 c baking powder
6 Tbsp caraway seeds
Melted butter for top

Mix together and bake at 350 degrees for 45 to 55 minutes.

Banana Nut Bread

Audrie Yoder-Fuchs/Bertha Hershberger

1/2 cube Butter
2 eggs
2 c sifted flour
1/2 tsp salt
1/2 c chopped nuts

1 c sugar
1 c mashed bananas (2 or 3)
1 tsp baking soda
1/3 c sour milk

Cream butter and sugar together. Add eggs and bananas, blend well. Sift flour, baking soda and salt together. Add to cream mixture alternately with the sour milk, beating. Smooth after each addition. Stir in nuts. Pour batter into greased loaf pan. Bake at 350 for 60 minutes. Remove from pan and cool on a wire rack.

Blueberry Muffins

Theme Buffet: **Big River** - *Chef Brenda Ritter*

1/2 c butter
1 1/4 c white sugar
1/2 c milk
1/2 tsp salt

2 c all-purpose flour
2 eggs
2 tsp baking powder
1 1/2 c fresh blueberries

Grease and flour muffin pan or use paper liners. Sift flour, baking powder and salt together and set aside. Cream butter and sugar until light and fluffy. Add eggs and beat well. Add milk and flour mixture. Beat until combined. Stir in blueberries. Fill muffin cups 2/3 full. Bake at 350 degrees for 25 to 30 minutes. Makes 1 dozen.

Braided Bread

Theme Buffet: **Smoke on the Mountain -** *Chef Brenda Ritter*

2 pkg yeast
6 Tbsp sugar
1/3 c vegetable oil
8 to 9 c flour
4 tsp poppy seeds or sesame seeds

2 1/2 c warm water
2 Tbsp salt
4 eggs, beaten
1 egg yolk mixed with 1 tsp water

Dissolve yeast in warm water in large bowl. Add sugar, salt, oil, and 6 cups of flour. Beat thoroughly with a wooden spoon. Gradually add more flour until dough is too stiff to beat with a spoon. Sprinkle some flour on a board and knead until dough is smooth (you may have to add a little more flour) and all flour is absorbed and the dough is no longer sticky. Knead by pushing the dough away from you folding in half and repeating. Place the dough in a large bowl and cover with a cloth. Let rise warm place (by the oven works well) for 1 1/2 hours, or as much time as the mixture needs to double in bulk. Punch down and divide the dough into 4 parts. Take each down and divide in three 9 inch strips, with the ends tapered smaller. Braid these 3 strips, and squeeze the ends to hold. Repeat with remaining parts. You can either place each loaf in a greased loaf pan, or place 2 loaves on a greased cookie sheet. Let rise again in warm spot, until dough has doubled in bulk (at least an hour). Then gently brush the tops with the egg mixture and sprinkle with seeds of choice. Bake in preheated oven at 375 degrees for 25 to 35 minutes or until loaves are golden brown. Cool on racks. Makes 4 loaves. Make this on a lazy weekend and then freeze extra. Place in the oven for a few minutes to freshen before serving. Leftovers make delicious toast or thick French toast!

Corn Muffins

Amish Acres Kitchen

1/2 c butter
1 egg
1 tsp salt
2 tsp cream of tartar
1 c flour

1/2 c sugar
1 c milk
1 tsp soda
1 c corn meal

Cream sugar and butter. Add remainder of ingredients. Mix well. Bake at 400 degrees for 20 to 25 minutes.

Butter Horns
Laura Slabaugh/Nancy Hershberger

1 pkg yeast
3 eggs
1/2 c sugar
1/2 tsp salt

1 Tbsp sugar
1 c water
1/2 c shortening
5 c flour

Mix yeast and sugar together. Beat in 3 eggs and water. Let set 15 minutes. Add sugar, shortening, salt and flour. Knead well. Divide into 2 parts and roll out in 12 inch circle. Cut and roll up starting with wide side. Let rise 3 or 4 hours. Bake at 400 for 15 minutes. Brush with butter.

Chiquita Banana Bread
Bertha Hershberger

1/3 c shortening
2 eggs, slightly beaten
2 3/4 tsp baking powder
1 c mashed bananas

2/3 c sugar
1 3/4 c flour
1/2 tsp salt
1/3 c nuts

Pour into a greased loaf pan. Bake at 350 for 60 to 70 minutes or until test done in the middle. Cool 20 to 30 minutes before removing from pan.

Cinnamon Rolls
Jacob and Loretta Kuhns, great-grandson of M.T. Kuhns

1 c mashed potatoes
1 c white sugar
1/2 c cream
3 beaten eggs
1 1/4 Tbsp yeast - dissolved in a little warm water
Flour enough to make a stiff dough

1 c lard
2 c scalded milk
1 tsp salt
1 tsp vanilla

Best if stirred together at night & put in fridge, worked out first thing in the morning. Let rise 1 to 2 hours before baking. Bake at 350 degrees for 15 to 20 minutes.

23

Cinnamon Twists
Mrs. John Mishler, great-grandson of M.T. Kuhns

1 c milk, scalded
1/2 c sugar
2 tsp salt
2 Tbsp yeast
1/2 c brown sugar
1/2 c margarine, melted

1 c warm water, divided
1/2 c vegetable oil
2 unbeaten eggs
8 c Robin Hood flour, approx.
2 tsp cinnamon

Dissolve yeast with 1 teaspoon sugar in 1/2 c. warm water. Let set 5 minutes or until bubbly. Beat eggs & remaining 1/2 c. warm water. Add scalded milk, oil, sugar, salt, & yeast mixture. Add 3 cups flour; beat well. Add remaining flour, just so it can be kneaded with hands. Knead well; cover & let rise 1 hour. Punch down & let rise again. Divide dough into 4 equal parts. On 2 well greased 12 inch pizza pan, pat 1/2 dough (1 part each) within 1 inch of rim. Brush with melted margarine. Combine brown sugar & cinnamon; divide between 2 pans, sprinkling evenly. Rollout remaining dough into 2 - 10 inch circles. Place each on top of cinnamon mixture, pressing edges to bottom dough. Brush top with margarine; sprinkle with cinnamon. Cut each circle into 4 sections from outside to center, not cutting within 1/2 inch, of center leaving all pieces connected. Now, cut each section into 4 pieces (like pie) to 1/2 inch of center. Do not cut through center. Pick up each piece & twist 3 or 4 times. Cover & let rise. Bake at 350 degrees for 15 to 20 minutes.

Glaze:
3 c powdered sugar
Hot water

Remaining margarine
1 tsp vanilla

Glaze: Pour remaining margarine into 3 cups powdered sugar. Add vanilla & hot water until thin enough to drizzle over warm rolls, moving in circles constantly. Yields 32 twists.

Dinner Rolls
Amish Acres Kitchen

3/4 c warm water
1 tsp sugar
1 c sugar
1/2 c butter

2 pkg yeast
2 c warm milk
4 eggs
7 to 8 c flour

Mix water, yeast and 1 tsp salt. Add milk, salt, sugar, eggs, butter and flour. Mix, let rise in pans. Bake at 350 until golden brown. Brush with butter or oil when removing from oven for a shine.

Dumplings
Susan Nunemaker

4 1/2 c flour
1 3/4 tsp baking powder

1 1/2 c milk
9 Tbsp shortening

Mix the first 3 ingredients, until looks like meal, stir in milk. Drop into hot meat juice. Cook uncovered for 10 minutes.

Easy Banana Bread
Angie Pletcher-Stillson

1 c sugar
1 egg
1 1/2 c flour

4 Tbsp butter
1 c mashed bananas
1/2 tsp soda

Cream sugar and butter, add eggs and beat until smooth. Add all other ingredients, mixing well. Bake in greased and floured loaf pan for 50 to 60 minutes at 350.

English Muffin Bread
Greg and Marsolie Kuhns, great-grandson of M.T. Kuhns

5 1/2 to 6 c flour
1 Tbsp sugar
1/4 tsp baking soda
1/2 c water

2 packages yeast
2 tsp salt
2 c milk

Combine 3 cups flour, yeast, sugar, salt, & soda. Heat liquids until warm (not hot). Add to dry mixture & beat well. Stir in more flour to make a stiff batter. Spoon into 2 WELL GREASED bread pans. Cover & let rise in a warm place for 45 minutes. Bake at 400 degrees for 25 minutes. REMOVE from pans IMMEDIATELY!! Great warm, cold, or toasted.

German Friendship Bread
Amish Acres Kitchen

Starter: Combine in large mixing bowl: 2 c all-purpose flour (unsifted), 1 tsp salt, 3 Tbsp sugar, 1 envelope dry yeast. Stir in 2 c very warm water until smooth paste forms. Cover with clean cloth, let stand in warm place (85 degrees) to sour and bubble for 2 or 3 days. Stir twice each day. (Keep starter in large jar or container, partially covered to allow gases to escape in refrigerator.) Stir down each day. When ready to bake cake, use 2 c starter and give 1 c to a friend along with a recipe.

DAY 1 - When a friend gives you the batter starter, place in large bowl, stir down and cover loosely with the waxed paper - leave on counter.
DAY 2, 3 & 4 - Stir batter until smooth
DAY 5 - Add 1 c flour, 1 c sugar and 1 c milk. Stir until smooth.
DAY 6, 7, 8 & 9 - Stir batter until smooth.
DAY 10 - Add 1 c flour, 1 c sugar and 1 c milk. Stir until smooth. Take out 3 separate cups of batter and give 1 cup each to three of your friends with the directions. To the remainder add: 2/3 c vegetable oil, 1 c sugar, 2 tsp baking powder, 3 eggs, 2 c flour, 1/2 tsp salt, 2 tsp vanilla, 1 1/2 tsp cinnamon, 1 1/2 tsp soda. Stir well by hand or by mixer on medium speed. Add any or all of the following: 1 c chopped nuts, 1 c apples and 1 c chopped raisins. Bake in greased and floured tube pan at 350 degrees for 45 to 55 minutes.

Golden Oatmeal Muffins
Bertha Hershberger

1 c flour
3 tsp baking powder
3 Tbsp vegetable oil
1 c milk

1/4 c sugar
1/2 tsp salt
1 egg beaten
1 c quick oats

Heat oven to 425. Sift together dry ingredients. Add liquids, stir only until moistened. Fill greased muffin cups 3/4 full. Bake 15 minutes.

Hillbilly Bread
Jacob and Loretta Kuhns, great-grandson of M.T. Kuhns

2 Tbsp honey
2/3 c brown sugar
1/2 c warm water w/4 Tbls yeast
2 c whole wheat flour

4 tsp salt
1/2 c oil
4 c warm water
10 to 11 c Robin Hood flour

Makes 5 loaves. Bake at 350 degrees for 23 minutes.

Jelly Roll
Martha Hochstetler, great-great granddaughter of M.T. Kuhns

4 eggs
Pinch of salt
1 c flour

1 Tbsp water
1 c sugar
1 tsp baking powder

Beat together eggs, water and salt. Add sugar, sift in flour and baking powder. Bake 5 to 10 minutes at 300 degrees. When done spread thickened fruit or pie filling on top. Roll while still hot.

Hot Cross Buns
Theme Buffet: **Brigadoon** - *Chef Brenda Ritter*

2 packages dry yeast
1 c milk
1/2 c sugar
1/4 tsp nutmeg
5 c flour
3 eggs

1/2 c warm water
1/2 c margarine or oil
1/2 tsp salt
3/4 c currants or raisins
1 tsp vanilla

Dissolve yeast in warm water. In large bowl combine milk, margarine, sugar, salt, nutmeg, vanilla, eggs and raisins. Stir in yeast mix. Gradually add flour mixing well after each addition. Turn out on floured board. Cover and let rest for 10 minutes. Knead until elastic, place in oiled bowl, turning so top is also oiled. Cover and let rise until doubled. Punch down. Turn out on floured board and flatten to about 1/2 inch. Cut with doughnut cutter and shape each into buns. Place on baking sheet. Brush will melted margarine. Cut cross on top of each bun, let rise until doubled. Bake at 375 degrees until brown. Ice with confectioners sugar icing or dust with confectioners sugar.

Icing:
1 c confectioners sugar

2 Tbsp water or lemon juice

Mix until smooth.

Mock Pizza Hut Pizza Dough
Freeman and Laura Schrock, great-great grandson M.T. Kuhns

2 pkgs or 2 Tbls yeast
2 tsp sugar
2 Tbsp vegetable oil
1 Tbsp salt
1/2 tsp oregano

2/3 c warm water
2 c cold water
2 Tbsp sugar
1/4 tsp garlic powder
6 1/2 c bread flour

Let first 3 ingredients stand until bubbly; set aside. Mix remaining ingredients, adding yeast mixture alternately with flour. Knead. Let rise until double. Place 1/4 c. vegetable oil (I don't use this much) in pan. Do not press up sides. Add pizza sauce only. Bake at 475 degrees for 15 minutes. Remove & add all your favorite toppings. Bake at 475 degrees for 10 minutes or until done. Makes 3 pizzas.

Navajo Fry Bread
Theme Buffet: **Annie Get Your Gun** - *Chef Brenda Ritter*

2 c flour	1 tsp salt
3 tsp baking powder	1 c water

Mix ingredients and let sit for 10 to 15 minutes. Break off a ball of dough about golf ball size and pat out no thicker than 1/4 inch. Fry in deep hot oil to a light golden brown, turn once to brown both sides. Drain bread well and pat with paper towel to remove excess oil. Keep covered in a bowl while cooking to keep bread warm. Can top with honey, powdered sugar or cinnamon.

Onion Bacon Biscuit Kuchen
Anne Stevens, great-granddaughter of M.T. Kuhns

2 to 3 c chopped onions	3 Tbsp butter
1/4 to 1/2 tsp salt	1/4 tsp black pepper
2 - 10 oz can flaky biscuits	1/2 c whipping cream
10 to 12 slices bacon (fried & crumbled)	3 eggs, slightly beaten
1/2 c shredded cheddar cheese	

Preheat oven to 375 degrees. Separate the dough into 20 biscuits and place in a 14" pizza pan (with sides) or a 9x13 cake pan, pressing dough over the bottom & 1" up the sides to form crust. Cook onions in butter in skillet until tender, but not browned. Stir in salt & pepper. Spoon onions over crust & sprinkle with the bacon. Combine eggs, sour cream, & cream until well blended: stir in cheese. Spoon evenly over onions & bacon. Sprinkle with additional pepper, if desired. Bake for 22 to 32 minutes, until crust is golden brown. Refrigerate leftovers. This recipe can be varied to your taste: Use sausage or ham instead of bacon: add green pepper, chives, chopped broccoli or parsley. Can assemble the night before & bake it in the morning.

Overnight Sticky Buns
Greg and Marsolie Kuhns, great-grandson of M.T. Kuhns

2 pkgs frozen roll dough   1 c brown sugar
2 small pkgs vanilla pudding mix (not instant)
2 Tbsp milk   2 tsp cinnamon
1 stick butter   1/2 c nuts, if desired

For a 9x13" pan use 1 1/2 pkgs roll dough. Put in bottom of well greased pan 5 balls wide. Heat on low, other ingredients, except nuts, until brown sugar is dissolved. Add nuts at this time. Pour over roll dough. Cover with waxed paper. (others will stick), and set on counter overnight. Bake at 350 degrees for 30 minutes. Invert into serving dish. Can be cut in half & made in 9 inch round cake pans.

Peanut Butter Muffins
Chris Townsend

1/4 c shortening   1/2 c sugar
1 egg   3 Tbsp peanut butter
1/2 c milk   3 Tbsp baking powder
1 Tbsp vanilla   1 c flour

Cream sugar and shortening. Add egg, peanut butter and milk. Add dry ingredients until just blended. Bake 20 to 25 minutes at 350 degrees.

Strawberry Bread
Nancy Hamman

1 c butter   1 1/2 c sugar
1 tsp vanilla   4 eggs
1 tsp salt   1 tsp baking soda
1 c strawberry jam   1/2 tsp lemon juice
3 c flour   1 tsp cream of tartar
1/2 c sour cream

Cream together butter and sugar. Add remainder of ingredients. Mix well. Bake in small bread pans. Bake at 350 for 50 to 55 minutes.

Pizza Dough
Martha A. Kuhns, great-granddaughter of M.T. Kuhns

2 Tbsp yeast
2/3 c warm water
2 Tbsp sugar
3 Tbsp vegetable oil
1/2 tsp oregano

2 tsp sugar
2 c cold water
3 c flour
1 Tbsp salt
1/4 tsp garlic salt or powder

Mix together yeast, 2 t. sugar and 2/3 c. warm water and let stand for 5 minutes. until bubbly. Mix rest of ingredients in separate bowl until smooth. Beat in yeast mixture. Add 3 1/2 c. more flour, work until elastic. Let rise until double. Put a little vegetable oil on pan and press dough into pan. Let rise 5 to 10 minutes. Add sauce & toppings, bake at 400 degrees for 10 to 15 min. I like to bake the crust for at least 5 minutes before putting sauce and topping on.

Pumpkin Bread
Wilma Kuhns, granddaughter of M.T. Kuhns

3 1/2 c flour
1 1/2 tsp salt
1 tsp nutmeg
1 c vegetable oil
2/3 c water
1/2 c chopped nuts (optional)

2 tsp soda
1 tsp cinnamon
3 c sugar
4 eggs, beaten
2 c canned pumpkin

Sift sugar, flour, salt and spices together. Make a "well" in dry ingredients and add the remaining ingredients. Mix well and bake one hour at 350 degrees. Makes 3 loaves.

Whole Wheat Bread
Mrs. David Lambright, great-grandson of M.T. Kuhns

4 c hot water
3/4 c brown sugar

1 c vegetable oil
2 Tbsp salt

5 c whole wheat flour
3 Tbsp yeast
4 c white flour

Mix together top four ingredients. Then add 5 c. whole wheat flour
and yeast. Let rise 20 minutes, then add 4 c. white flour.
If more flour is needed add more wheat flour. Bake at 350 degrees
for 15 minutes then turn down to 300 degrees for 30 minutes.
Makes 4 big loaves or 5 small loaves.

Zucchini Bread
Audrie Yoder-Fuchs

3 eggs
1 c oil
3 tsp vanilla
3 c flour
1 tsp salt
1/4 t baking powder

2 c sugar
2 c grated zucchini
1/2 c nuts
1 tsp baking soda
1 tsp cinnamon

Beat eggs and add sugar, oil and zucchini and vanilla.
Then add remaining ingredients. Bake at 350 degrees for 1 hour
or until done.

Soups
& Salads

A Salad That's Different
Jonathan Mishler, great-grandson of M.T. Kuhns

1 pt small curd cottage cheese
1 - 8 oz carton whipped topping
1 can crushed pineapple or fruit cocktail
1 - 3 oz package Jell-O, your choice of flavor

Mix cheese and well drained fruit until well blended. Sprinkle dry Jell-O over fruit mixture and stir well. Fold in whipped topping. Refrigerate 3 to 4 hours before serving.

Beet Pickles
Audrie Yoder-Fuchs

2 c sugar
1 Tbsp whole all spice
3 1/2 c vinegar
3 oz beets, peeled & cooked

1 1/2 tsp salt
2 sticks cinnamon
1 1/2 c water

Wash and drain beets. Cover with boiling water cook until tender. Combine all ingredients, except beets. Simmer 15 minutes. Pack beets into hot ball jar, leave 1/2 inch head space. Remove cinnamon. Bring liquid to boil. Pour boiling water over beets.

Brizola Marinade
Theme Buffet: Zorba - Chef Brenda Ritter

8 oz red wine
2 oz lemon juice
1 tsp salt

6 oz olive oil
2 garlic cloves, minced
1 tsp pepper

Combine and pour over meat. Refrigerate.
Great for beef cubes or kabobs.

Broccoli Salad
Michan Eby

Salad

4 heads broccoli, diced

12 slices bacon, fried and crumbled

1 c raisins (optional)

1 medium onion, diced

1 c sunflower seeds (or less)

Dressing

1 c mayonnaise

1 or 2 Tbsp vinegar

1/2 c sugar

Mix dressing and pour over other ingredients.

Broccoli/Cauliflower Salad
Laura Slabaugh

1 head cabbage, chopped fine

1 head broccoli, broken

1 lb bacon, fried and broken

1 1/2 c shredded cheese

1 head cauliflower, broken

1 onion, chopped fine

Dressing

2 c mayonnaise

1/2 c sugar

Mix well and serve.

Broken Glass Jell-O
Marilyn Yoder, great-granddaughter of M.T. Kuhns

1 box Jell-O each of blue, green, orange, & red

2 boxes lemon Jell-O

2 - 8 oz cream cheese

2 c hot water

16 oz Cool Whip

Dissolve first 4 Jell-O's separately in 1 cup boiling water. Pour in sandwich boxes to set. In large bowl dissolve lemon Jell-O in hot water. Add cream cheese to soften. When Jell-O's have set firm, cut into small pieces & fold into the lemon mixture after it has set a little & cool whip has been added. This makes enough for 2 Jell-O molds.

Buttermint Salad
Ruth Ann Miller

2 - 13 oz Crushed pineapple, undrained   1 package dry lime Jell-O
1 - 7 oz soft buttermints, crusted   1 - 9 oz cool whip
1 - 10 oz package miniature marshmallows

Mix pineapple, Jell-O and marshmallows in a large bowl. Cover and refrigerate overnight. Add mints and cool whip in morning and serve. Pour into large bowl and refrigerate. Serve chilled.

Capitol Salad
Susie Pletcher

1 head of lettuce, Romaine or Spinach
1/2 to 1 c chopped celery   3 to 4 green onions, chopped
1 can mandarin oranges   1/3 c toasted almonds

Dressing
1/4 c oil   2 Tbsp sugar
2 Tbsp tarragon vinegar   1/4 tsp Tabasco
1/2 tsp salt

Mix salad ingredients together top with dressing.

Carrot Pennies
Verda Hochstetler

2 lbs baby carrots (slices)   1 large onion (cut-up)
1 large green pepper (raw and diced)   1 c sugar
1 can cream of tomato soup   1/2 c vinegar
1/2 tsp salt   1 tsp dry mustard
1 tsp Worcestershire sauce   1/2 c salad oil

Boil baby carrots in salt water until slightly tender. Add green pepper and onion. In a separate pan mix cream of tomato soup, sugar, vinegar, salt, dry mustard, Worcestershire sauce and salad oil. Heat and pour over carrot mixture. Refrigerate for 24 hours before serving.

Cauliflower Salad
David Mishler, great-great-grandchild of M.T. Kuhns

2 heads lettuce
1 chopped onion
1/2 c cheddar cheese shredded
1/2 c chopped carrots

1 head cauliflower
1 lb bacon
1/2 c chopped celery

Dressing
2 c salad dressing
2 tsp sour cream & onion mix

1/2 c sugar

Put dressing on salad about 1/2 hour before serving.

Cottage Cheese Salad
Ivan and Susie Kuhns, grandson of M.T. Kuhns

1 box lime Jell-O
2 c hot water
1 c cottage cheese
1 c whipped topping

1 box lemon Jell-O
1 c crushed pineapple
1/3 c salad dressing

Dissolve Jell-O in boiling water, add pineapple.
Let cool until slightly jelled then add cottage cheese,
salad dressing and whipped cream.

Cranberry Relish Salad
Verda Hochstetler

1 - 3 oz package strawberry Jell-O
1 1/2 c sugar
1 med apple - peeled (Apple & Cranberries need to be chopped and prepared ahead of time)
1/2 c orange juice (concentrate)

1 c boiling water
1 pkg (12 oz) cranberries

1/2 c pecans (chopped)

Dissolve Jell-O in boiling water. Add and mix sugar, cranberries,
apple, orange juice and pecans. Pour in a 1 1/2 qt dish and
refrigerate for 4 hours.

37

Cous Cous Salad
Theme Buffet: Smoke on the Mountain - *Chef Brenda Ritter*

Cous Cous
Water, same amount as cous cous
1 tsp salt
Spinach

1 tsp curry powder
Walnuts

Apple Layer
12 Granny Smith apples with skin
8 oz of butter melted in skillet

2 Tbsp cinnamon
1 Tbsp curry mix

Add apples to mixture. Cook 5 minutes, let cool.
Bring water to a boil, add cous cous. Stir, turn off heat and let sit for 15 minutes. Put cous cous on leaking sheet and let it slightly brown. Put in pan by layers: Walnuts on each layer.
Spinach layer - cous cous layer - apple layer - repeat.

Cranberry Salad
Amish Acres Kitchen

1/2 lb cranberries
1 1/2 c sugar
2 oranges or 1/2 c crushed pineapple
1 pkg cherry or strawberry Jell-O

3 apples
1/4 c chopped walnuts
1 c cold water
1 c hot water

Wash and grind cranberries through food chopper. Pare and core apples and chop very fine. Add chopped oranges, nuts and sugar. Dissolve Jell-O in hot water. Add cold water. When cool, add salad mix.

Five Cup Salad
Sherry Maurer

1 c pineapple chunks, drained
1 c miniature marshmallows
1/2 c chopped pecans (optional)

1 c coconut
1 c mandarin oranges, drained
1 c sour cream

Mix all ingredients, chill several hours or overnight. Freezes well.

Dilled Chicken Salad
Andrea Stahly

1 pkg spiral pasta, cooked & drained	2 c cubed cooked chicken
1/3 c chopped onion, optional	1 c chopped celery
1 - 10 oz pkg thawed frozen peas, optional	

In a large bowl, combine ingredients, mix well.

Dressing

1 - 10 oz envelope ranch dressing mix	
2 c sour cream	1 c mayonnaise
1 c milk	1/2 tsp garlic salt
3 Tbsp minced fresh dill or 1 Tbsp dill weed	

Combine dressing ingredients, whisk until smooth. Pour over salad, toss to coat. Cover and refrigerate for at least 2 hours.

Dimas Greek Greens
Theme Buffet: Triumph of Love - Chef Brenda Ritter

Romaine	Arugula
Dandelion Greens	Boston Bibb Lettuce
Red Cabbage	Spinach

Dressing

1 c oil	1/3 c catsup
1/4 c vinegar	1 small onion quartered
2 tsp salt	2 tsp paprika
2/3 c sugar	

In a blender combine all dressing ingredients. Blend thoroughly.

French Dressing
Mrs. Freeman Mishler, great-grandchild of M.T. Kuhns

2 c salad dressing	1 1/2 c sugar
1/4 c vinegar	1/2 c ketchup
2 tsp mustard	1 tsp paprika
1/2 tsp salt	4 tsp water
1/2 c cooking oil	

Fresh Fruit Compote
Theme Buffet: Hello, Dolly! - *Chef Brenda Ritter*

1 cantaloupe, cut in chunks	1 honeydew, cut in chunks
1 qt strawberries, sliced	1 qt blueberries
4 kiwi, sliced	1/2 c sherry

Mix in layers, drizzle with sherry.

Frozen Fruit Salad
Angie Pletcher-Stillson

12 oz can frozen orange juice	1/2 c sugar
1 large can crushed pineapple	1 large can fruit cocktail
1 small can mandarin oranges	2 c blueberries
3 to 4 bananas, sliced	

Mix orange juice and sugar in a 9x13 inch tupperware. Pour in undrained fruit cans. Cover and freeze. You can also use clear plastic tumblers or Dixie cups to freeze individual portions.

Garden Salad
Verda Hochstetler

1 head of lettuce (broken up)	1 onion (cut fine)
1 c celery (cut up)	1 pkg frozen peas
2 c salad dressing	2 tsp sugar

Mix together in a shallow pan the lettuce, onion, celery and peas. Mix together the salad dressing and sugar. Spread this on top of lettuce mixture. Sprinkle 4 oz of parmesan cheese on dressing dotted with 8 slices of bacon, cut up and fried. Refrigerate for 24 hours.

Gram's Confetti Salad
Andrea Stahly

2 heads of lettuce
1 sm pint salad tomatoes
1 can mandarin oranges, well drained
1 c pineapple tidbits, well drained
1 large bottle ranch dressing
1 sm red, yellow and/or green peppers, chopped

1/2 c celery chopped
1 c red and/or green grapes
1 med bag salad crotons
1 med pkg of cheddar cheese

Tear up lettuce into bite size pieces, put into a large bowl.
Add peppers, celery. Whole salad tomatoes, oranges and pineapple.
(Ingredients can be altered to taste.) Toss salad in large bowl.
The salad dressing, cheese and crotons are best when added just
before serving to guests.

Grape Salad
Jacob and Loretta Kuhns, great-grandson of M.T. Kuhns

4 lbs red seedless grapes
8 oz sour cream
1 1/2 c powdered sugar

8 oz package cream cheese
8 oz Cool Whip

Mix well. Add grapes. Chill. (Don't cut grapes)

Harlequin Gelatin Salad
Theme Buffet: Triumph of Love - Chef Brenda Ritter

2 pkgs Jell-O (any flavor) with fruit of your choice.
8 oz pkg cream cheese   1/2 c powdered sugar

Cut Jell-O into diamond shaped pieces. In a separate mixing bowl
mix cream cheese and powdered sugar until well mixed and soft.
Toss in Jell-O pieces.

Lancaster Field Greens
Theme Buffet: 1776 - *Chef Brenda Ritter*

4 bunches mustard greens or turnip greens
1 finely chopped small onion   1 bunch beet tops
Butter and/or vinegar for seasoning   Salt pork, if desired
Salt and pepper to taste

Prepare greens for cooking by cutting off the tough part of the stems and washing them in cold water several times until thoroughly free of grit, then let them sit in cold water for 1 hour. Boil greens, beet tops and onion (and salt pork, if desired) in small amount of salted water for 1 hour. Drain well, season with salt and pepper and a little butter and/or vinegar.

Olive Oil Dressing
Theme Buffet: Man of La Mancha - *Chef Brenda Ritter*

1/2 c chopped shallots   2 Tbsp crushed garlic
1 small chopped onion   1 tsp salt
1 tsp pepper   2 c olive oil, extra virgin
1 c vinegar

Combine and shake until well mixed.

Orange Tapioca Salad
Rhoda Hershberger

1 box instant vanilla pudding   1 box instant tapioca
1 box orange Jell-O   3 c water

Combine ingredients and bring to a rolling boil. Cool.
Stir in 1 cup cool whip and 1 can drained mandarin oranges.
Chill.

Poppy Seed Dressing
Ruth Ann Miller

3/4 c sugar
1/3 c vinegar
1 tsp salt
2 tsp prepared mustard

5 tsp onion
2 tsp poppy seed
1 1/4 c salad oil
3/4 c sour cream

Mix sugar, salt, onion, oil, vinegar and prepared mustard in blender. Add poppy seed and sour cream till blended.

Potato Salad
Verda Hochstetler

8 medium size potatoes
5 hard boiled eggs (cut up)
1/3 c sweet pickles (optional)

1 medium size onion
1/2 c celery (cut up)

Dressing
2 c mayonnaise
1/4 tsp salt
2 1/4 tsp vinegar

3/4 c sugar
3 Tbsp mustard

Peel, cook, cool and shred potatoes. Mix in onion, boiled eggs, celery and sweet pickles. Pour dressing over potato mixture. Best if prepared several hours in advance so flavors can blend. Put in tight containers.

Potato Salad
Greg and Marsolie Kuhns, great-grandson of M.T. Kuhns

8 medium potatoes
3 to 4 hard cooked eggs
1 1/2 c real mayonnaise
Salt & pepper to taste

1 small onion, chopped
1 Tbsp dill relish
1 Tbsp horseradish sauce

Peel, dice, & cook potatoes until tender; drain. Mix in mayonnaise, horseradish, onion, celery, & relish. Add salt & pepper. Then cut up eggs & mix in well. Chill.

Pretty Pink Salad
Edna Yoder, granddaughter of M.T. Kuhns

16 large marshmallows
1 - 8 oz package cream cheese
1 - 3 oz package red Jell-O
1 - 13 oz can crushed pineapples and juice

1/4 c milk
2 c Cool Whip

Heat pineapple, juice, Jell-o and marshmallows until marshmallows are melted. Set aside to cool. In a big bowl beat cream cheese and milk until smooth. Fold in whipped cream. When Jell-o mixture has cooled combine the 2 mixtures and pour into serving dish or mold. Refrigerate until set.

Rice Salad
Mrs. Jerry Kuhns, grandson of M.T. Kuhns

1 c uncooked rice
4 or 5 eggs hardboiled & diced
1 c sweet pickles or relish
1 c salad dressing or mayonnaise
1 1/2 Tbsp prepared mustard

1 1/2 c celery diced
1/4 c sugar
Pinch of salt
Onions - optional

Cook rice in 1 quart salt water until tender, drain in strainer, & run cold water over it to cool. Then add the remaining ingredients.

Spicy Red Cabbage
Theme Buffet: **My Fair Lady -** *Chef Brenda Ritter*

5 c shredded red cabbage
1/2 c raisins
1/4 c water
2 Tbsp vinegar
3/4 tsp salt
1 tsp mixed spices tied in wet cheesecloth (optional)

1 c diced apple
1/2 c chopped onion
2 Tbsp butter
2 Tbsp sugar
Dash of pepper

Place all ingredients in slow cooker, cover. Cook on low for 6 to 8 hours or on high for 3 to 4 hours. Stir occasionally.

Spinach Salad
Rhoda Hershberger

Salad

12 oz pkg fresh spinach	4 hard boiled eggs, chopped
1 can sliced water chestnuts	8 oz fresh mushrooms, sliced
Bacon - fried and crumbled	Alfalfa sprouts
Shredded cheese	

Combine and toss. When serving garnish with chow mien noodles. Can also use 1/2 lettuce and 1/2 spinach instead of all spinach.

Dressing

3/4 c sugar	1 c vinegar
1 tsp worcestershire sauce	1/3 c ketchup
1 med onion, chopped	

Mix dressing ingredients well. Blend 1 cup dressing into salad.

Stuffed Grape Leaves
Theme Buffet: Zorba - *Chef Brenda Ritter*

1 oz chopped garlic	12 oz onion, fine dice
4 oz olive oil	12 oz rice, uncooked
20 oz puree tomatoes	1/2 tsp salt
1/4 tsp pepper	1 oz chopped parsley
1 oz pine nuts, roasted	50 grape leaves, rinsed
1 qt vegetable stock	3 oz lemon juice

Cook garlic and onion until tender in olive oil. Add rice, stir to coat with oil. Add tomato, salt and pepper. Combine and heat through. Remove from pan, mix in parsley and pine nuts. Cool and reserve. Place grape leaves in sauce pan with water to cover. Bring to boil, blanch until softened. Spread each leave on a flat surface. Place 1 T. of rice mixture in center of each leaf, roll like and egg roll. Place a rack on bottom of braising vessel. Place the rolls side by side on top rack, cover with stock and lemon juice, use a weighted place to keep them submerged. Braise on top of stove for 1 hour. Cool overnight. Serve chilled.

Sweet & Sour Cabbage Salad
Amish Acres Thresher Dinner

6 lb of cabbage, chopped	1 1/8 c sugar
1/2 c vinegar	1/2 c oil
1/8 tsp seasoning salt	1/4 tsp salt
Dash celery salt	1/2 pimento, chopped

Chop cabbage, peeling off outer leaves and quartering.
Run through minimum times so cabbage is uneven.
Add rest of ingredients to cabbage. Mix well.

Taffy Apple Salad
Gloria Fimbianti

1 lg can pineapple tidbits, drained, save juice

2 c mini marshmallows	1/2 c sugar
1 egg, well beaten	1 - 8 oz Cool Whip
1 1/2 c salted cocktail peanuts	1 Tbsp flour
1 1/2 Tbsp white vinegar	2 c diced, unpeeled apples

Mix pineapple and marshmallows; refrigerate overnight. Take juice,
flour, sugar, vinegar and egg; cook until thick. Refrigerate overnight
also. **Next day:** Mix cool whip with the sauce. Add marshmallows
and pineapple mixture to this, then the apples and peanuts.
Make sure it is well mixed.

Waldorf Salad
Theme Buffet: Hello, Dolly! - Chef Brenda Ritter

2 apples	3 stalk celery, chopped
1/4 c mayonnaise	3/4 c raisins
Drop of lemon juice and sugar	1/2 c walnuts

Cut apples into bite size pieces. Add raisins and nuts.
Mix mayonnaise, lemon juice and sugar then add to apple mixture.

Three Layer Salad
Bertha Kuhns, great-granddaughter of M.T. Kuhns

2 boxes Jell-O any flavor lime & lemon are good
3 3/4 c hot water   8 oz cream cheese
1 c drained, crushed pineapple   1 c cream, whipped
1/2 c sugar

Mix Jell-O & water. Add pineapple let stand till firm. Whip cream then add cream cheese, 1/2 cup sugar whip together & spread on first layer.

1 c sugar   2 Tbsp flour
2 eggs   1 c pineapple juice

Cook till thick: last 4 ingredients & put on second layer.

Tortellini Salad
Gloria Fimbianti

1/3 c vegetable oil   2 tsp dijon style mustard
3 c cooked cheese filled tortellini   2 c cooked broccoli flowerets
1 1/2 c sliced fresh mushrooms   1 1/2 c halved cherry tomatoes
1 c chopped zesty dill spears   Fresh basil for garnish
1/2 tsp dried basil leaves, crushed   2 Tbsp wine vinegar

To make dressing: In small bowl, combine oil, vinegar, mustard and basil. In large bowl, combine tortellini, broccoli, mushrooms, tomatoes and pickles. Add dressing; toss gently to coat. Cover and refrigerate until serving time, at least 4 hours.

Warm Potato Salad
Theme Buffet: **The Sound of Music -** *Chef Brenda Ritter*

4 potatoes
1 tsp sugar
Salt and pepper to taste
1 diced cucumber

3 egg yolks
1 tsp celery seed
1 diced onion
1 c vinegar

Boil the potatoes, let cool, pare and dice. Beat the egg yolks, mix with salt, pepper, sugar and celery seed, bring to a boil. Remove from heat and add to potatoes. Add the diced onion and cucumber, then the vinegar. Serve immediately.

White Jell-O
Gloria Fimbianti

8 oz softened cream cheese
1 package Knox gelatin
1 c milk
1 c crushed pineapple, drained
1 c whipped cream or 8 oz. Cool whip

1/2 c sugar (optional)
1/2 c water
1 t vanilla
1 Tbsp lime juice

Mix cream cheese in sugar. In small bowl, sprinkle gelatin over 1/3 c water; set bowl in pan of water and heat until dissolved. Beat into cream cheese mixture, milk vanilla and lime juice. Add gelatin mixture to Jell-O and crushed pineapple. Fold whipped cream into combined mixtures. Pour into 4 cup mold and chill until set. Substitutes for pineapple: thawed frozen strawberries or raspberries.

Chili
Bertha Hershberger

1 lb hamburger
1 c tomato paste
2 cans water
Salt & pepper to taste

1 chopped onion
1 c tomato soup
2 cans chili beans

Mix all ingredients together. Simmer one hour.

Bean Soup
Amish Acres Thresher Dinner

1 lb soup beans
1/2 c chopped onion
1/2 tsp celery salt
Salt and pepper

1 ham bone
1/2 tsp seasoning salt
Dash of garlic salt

Soak beans in water overnight. Drain, add fresh water and cook slowly with the ham bone for 2 hours. Add onion, celery salt, seasoning salt and garlic salt, salt and pepper. Remove ham bone, trim off any meat and return to pot, add ham bits and simmer for 1 hour.

Cheeseburger Chowder
Mary E. Miller, granddaughter of M.T. Kuhns

1 lb hamburger, browned & drained
1 small onion
2 1/2 c milk
1 c cheddar cheese

2 medium potatoes
1/2 tsp salt
3 Tbsp flour

In 3 qt. saucepan cook potatoes, celery, onion and salt in 1 1/2 c. water until tender. Add browned hamburger and 2 c. milk. Use remaining 1/2 c milk to blend with flour. Cook until thickened. Add cheese.

Clam Chowder
Theme Buffet: Hello, Dolly! - *Chef Brenda Ritter*

1 clove garlic, minced
2 oz butter
2 c water
2 Tbsp salt
2 c heavy cream
2 Tbsp flour

1 large onion, diced
2 c soft shell clams and juice
1/4 tsp thyme
1/8 tsp pepper
1 1/2 c diced potatoes
2 Tbsp butter

Sauté onion in 2 oz. butter until crisp. Add garlic and clams, bring to a boil, then add vegetables. Add cream. Melt butter and add flour to butter. Add to clam mixture to thicken.

Cock-a-leekie Soup
Theme Buffet: **Brigadoon** - *Chef Brenda Ritter*

12 prunes, soaked overnight (optional)   1 lb leeks, trimmed and sliced
2.5 lb oven ready fresh chicken   2 pint water
2 chicken stock cubes   Bouquet garni
Salt & freshly ground black pepper   Chopped parsley to garnish
Corn flour (to thicken if necessary)

Dissolve the stock cubes in water and add to large pan with the bouquet garni, chicken and leeks. Bring to the boil and remove any scum. Simmer very gently for 1 to 1.5 hours until the chicken is tender. Remove chicken from the pan, skin it and cut the meat into neat portions. Return it to the pan. If using prunes, add now and simmer for 20 minutes. Thicken with a little corn flour mixed to a cream with water, add parsley. Flavor improves if this dish is made the night before serving.

Homemade Cheese Soup
Andrea Stahly

2 c water   2 c diced potatoes
1/2 c diced carrots   1/2 c chopped celery
1/4 c finely chopped onion   1 1/2 tsp salt
1/4 tsp pepper   1 c cubed fully cooked ham

In a large sauce pan, combine first 7 ingredients. Bring to a boil. Reduce heat cover and simmer until vegetables are tender. Add ham.

1/4 c margarine   1/4 c all-purpose flour
2 c milk   2 c shredded cheddar cheese

In another sauce pan, melt the butter, stir in flour until smooth. Gradually add milk. Bring to a boil; cook and stir for 2 minutes or until thickened. Stir in cheese until melted; add to the soup.

Egg Drop Soup
Bertha Hershberger

3 c chicken broth
2 Tbsp cold water
1 egg, beaten

1 Tbsp cornstarch
1 onion, chopped

Heat chicken broth to 400 degrees in saucepan. Reduce to simmer. Dissolve cornstarch in water. Add and stir until slightly thickened; then add onion and egg. Serve immediately.

Fresh Asparagus Soup
Gloria Fimbianti

1/2 lb. fresh asparagus, cut in 1/4" slices
2 1/2 Tbsp chicken soup concentrate
1 c chopped carrots
1/2 c celery
1/3 c flour
1 tsp salt
1 Tbsp lemon juice

1/2 c chopped onion
3 Tbsp butter, softened
5 c warm water
Dash pepper

In medium size pot mix flour into softened butter.
Add water to smooth paste. Add chicken concentrate and seasonings, simmer 10 minutes. Add chopped vegetables and cook until veggies are tender.

Hearty Hamburger Soup
Mrs. Albert Miller, granddaughter of M.T. Kuhns

2 Tbsp butter
1 lb hamburger
1 c onions, diced
1 c potatoes, diced
1/8 tsp pepper
1/3 c flour

1 c sliced carrots
2 c tomato juice
1/2 c celery, diced
1 1/2 tsp salt
1 tsp seasoned salt
4 c milk

Brown meat, add vegetables, juice, & seasonings, cover & simmer till vegetables are tender. Combine flour & 1 cup milk, stir into soup. Boil, add remaining milk to almost boiling point, but do not boil.

Lentil Soup
Theme Buffet: Zorba - *Chef Brenda Ritter*

1 lb lentils, rinsed and picked through
10 c water (or substitute half with chicken stock)
1 large onion, chopped
2 c celery, chopped (tops & all)
1/2 tsp pepper

3 tsp salt
1 lb sweet Italian sausage
3 large carrots, diced
1 tsp oregano
1 c tomato sauce

Combine the lentils and water. Bring to boil for 2 minutes. Remove from heat and let stand for 1 hour to soften. Return lentils and water to heat. Bring to boil. Add 2 t. salt and simmer for 1 hour. Brown sausage, add to lentils. Sauté chopped onion in the sausage drippings, pouring off most of the fat first. Add carrots and celery, cook for 2 min. Stir in remaining salt with oregano and pepper into vegetables. Add this mixture to the kettle of lentils. Stir in tomato sauce. Simmer 30 minutes longer.

Okra Soup
Amish Acres Kitchen

1/2 lb okra
1 c chopped onions
1/2 c minced green peppers
2 c roughly chopped, peeled and seeded tomatoes (or use canned)
7 c chicken stock
1 c lima beans
1 to 1 1/2 c minced chicken

3 Tbsp butter
1/2 c chopped celery
1/2 c minced carrots (optional)
1/2 c uncooked rice
2 c corn kernels
Salt and pepper to taste

Wash, dry, and de-stem okra into 1/4 inch slices. Heat Butter in a very large saucepan. Cook onions, celery, peppers, and carrots until wilted, 5 to 10 minutes. Add okra, sauté for 5 minutes, stirring until the "roping" of the okra juices diminishes. Add tomatoes and chicken stock. Bring to a boil, stir in rice, reduce heat, cover, and simmer for 10 minutes. Add lima beans and simmer for 10 more minutes. Add corn and chicken; heat through for approximately 5 minutes. Season to taste and serve. Makes 2 quarts.

Quick Golden Stew
Rhoda Hershberger

1 1/2 c potatoes, peeled & diced
2 med onions, chunked
2 c cubed ham
1 jar process cheese spread

4 medium carrots
10 oz raw peas
1 c cream of celery soup

In large saucepan combine carrots, potatoes, and onions with just enough water to cover. Cover and cook until veggies are tender, approx. 10 min. Add peas and ham, cook 5 more minutes. Drain water, stir in soup and cheese. Heat through and serve.

Roasted Tomato and Carrot Soup
Theme Buffet: Fiddler on the Roof - *Chef Brenda Ritter*

2 lbs Roma tomatoes
1/2 cup dried onion
1 tsp thyme
1/2 tsp pepper

1/2 c olive oil
1 lb baby carrots
3 Tbsp chicken base
1/2 gallon water

Coat baking pan with olive oil. Quarter tomatoes, brush with olive oil. Roast in 350 degree oven for 20 to 25 minutes. Let cool, remove skins. Put onions in pot with olive oil. Brown, add rest of ingredients. Simmer 1 hour.

Sitting Bull's Dried Corn Soup
Theme Buffet: Annie Get Your Gun - *Chef Brenda Ritter*

3 c dried corn
1/2 lb cubed pork (or beef)
1 clove minced garlic
1/2 tsp oregano
1/2 tsp black pepper

12 c water
1 diced onion
6 crushed red chili pods
3 tsp salt

Wash dried corn thoroughly, soak overnight, drain when ready to use. Boil dried corn until tender - about 3 1/2 hours in 6 cups water. Brown meat, add onion and garlic, sauté together until tender, drain off excess fat. Add pork, chili pods, oregano, salt, pepper and 6 cups water to cooked corn. Simmer for 1 hour or until the meat and corn are tender. Makes 2 quarts.

© Amish Acres, Nappanee, Indiana

Steak Soup
Gloria Fimbianti

1 stick oleo	1 c flour
1/2 gallon Water	2 lb ground beef, drained
1 c onion	1 c celery
1 c carrots	2 c frozen mixed vegetables
Barley	1/2 can tomatoes
2 Tbsp beef base concentrate	1 tsp black pepper

Melt oleo and whip in 1 c. flour to make a smooth paste. Stir in water. Sauté ground beef, drain off grease and add to soup. Add veggies, beef base and pepper. Bring to a boil. Reduce to simmer for 1 hour or until veggies and barley are tender.

Swiss Cheese Soup
Theme Buffet: **Meet Me in St. Louis** - *Chef Brenda Ritter*

1 Tbsp butter	2 oz flour
10 oz chicken stock (or can of chicken broth)	21 oz milk
8 oz processed cheese food	8 oz swiss cheese, shredded
Salt & white pepper	10 oz Sauterne wine

Melt butter in sauce pan and slowly add flour to make a roux. Add milk and chicken stock, stirring constantly. Bring to boil and let simmer for 15 minutes. Stir in cheese food and Swiss cheese, stirring constantly, simmer for 5 minutes.
Add salt, pepper and seasoning. Just before serving add Sauterne wine - simmer 1 minute.

West Indies Pepperpot Soup
Theme Buffet: 1776 - Chef Brenda Ritter

1 lb tripe, cubed	1 lb stewing beef, cubed
2 qts water	1 onion, diced
1/3 c celery, diced	1/4 c green pepper, diced
4 Tbsp fat	4 Tbsp flour
2 potatoes, diced	1 Tbsp salt

Cover meat with cold water and bring to a boil. Sauté onion, celery and pepper in fat for 15 min. Add flour, stir until blended. Add meat, stock, potatoes and seasonings. Simmer for 1 hour.

Turkey Chowder
Ruth Ann Miller

2 frozen turkey wings	1 Tbsp salt
1 medium onion	1 c carrots
1 c celery	1 c potatoes
6 Tbsp flour	1 c shredded mild cheese
2 c milk	1/4 c butter

Place wings in large pan, add water until wings are just covered. Add salt and onion. Bring to boil. Reduce heat and simmer for 2 1/2 hours or until meat is tender. Remove wings from broth. Remove meat from bones and cut in small pieces, set aside. To 4 cups broth (add water if needed) add carrots, celery, potatoes simmer until tender. Stir in turkey gradually blend milk into flour until smooth, stir into broth along with, butter and cheese. Cook over medium heat, stirring constantly until thickened. Season to taste. I would wait to add my meat until after it is thick.

Vegetables

Baked Sweet Potato Casserole
Lenore Pletcher

Sweet potatoes   Salt
Brown sugar   Raisins
Butter   Small marshmallows

Boil sweet potatoes and drain. Then peel and mash. Add salt, brown sugar, butter, and raisins to taste. Put in baking dish. Bake at 350 degrees, 30 to 40 minutes. Before serving, put marshmallows on the top, and put back in the oven to brown. Serve with Thanksgiving or any other special meal.

Bread Dressing
Amish Acres Thresher Dinner

18 slices of toasted or stale bread   1 c chopped celery
1/2 c chopped onions   1 tsp seasoning salt
1/2 tsp poultry salt   1 Tbsp sage
3 beaten eggs   1 qt liquid, preferably stock

Put all ingredients in large mixing bowl. Add beaten eggs, stock. Mix well. Add turkey or chicken bits if available. Put in baking dish. Bake at 350 until done.

Broccoli Casserole
Greg and Marsolie Kuhns, great-grandson of M.T. Kuhns

1 - 16 oz pkg frozen broccoli   2 c shredded cheddar cheese
1 can cream of mushroom soup   1 c bread crumbs
1 Tbsp real prepared horseradish

Cook broccoli according to package directions. Mix together soup, cheese, & horseradish. Pour over broccoli into buttered 2 quart casserole. Top with bread crumbs. Bake at 350 degrees for 45 minutes.

© Amish Acres, Nappanee, Indiana

Broccoli Rice Casserole
Nancy Hamman

2 pkgs frozen broccoli, chopped & thawed
1/2 stick oleo
2 c rice, cooked
1/2 c milk
1 c shredded cheese

1 med onion, chopped
2 cans creamed soup, any kind
1/2 c miracle whip

Mix and bake at 350 degrees in a 9 x 13 inch pan for 1 1/2 hours.

California Blend Casserole
Mary Etta Kuhns, great-granddaughter of M.T. Kuhns

1 pkg frozen California Blend vegetables
1 small can mushroom soup
1 roll Ritz crackers, crushed
1 can sliced chestnuts, optional

8 oz Velveeta cheese, sliced
1 stick margarine

Mix all vegetables with soup and cheese. Do not dilute soup. Sprinkle with crackers and drizzle margarine. Bake at 350 degrees for 45 minutes.

Candied Mashed Yams
Stephanie Yoder

4 fresh yams
1 bag of miniature marshmallows
3 Tbsp orange juice
3 Tbsp pineapple juice (or 1/4 orange juice instead of using pineapple juice)

3 Tbsp butter
1/4 c brown sugar
Walnuts

Cook yams, drain, and discard juice. Peel off skins and mash by hand or mixer. Add butter, brown sugar, and juice. For a creamier mixture add more butter, for a sweeter mixture add more juice. Put into a small casserole dish and top with marshmallows. In a skillet melt 2 or 3 pats of butter, add walnuts and coat with butter. Add small amounts of brown sugar to the mixture to candy the walnuts. Sprinkle these on top and put in the oven at 350 degrees until the marshmallows melt, let cool slightly and serve. May fold walnuts into mashed yams for a different effect.

Cheese Potatoes
Nancy Hamman

1 large pkg hashbrowns, thawed	1 stick melted oleo
1 large sour cream, optional	2 c cream of chicken soup
8 oz shredded cheese	1 tsp salt

Mix all ingredients together and pour in a 9 x 13 inch pan. Bake at 350 degrees for 45 to 60 minutes.

Cheesy Rice
Greg and Marsolie Kuhns, great-grandson of M.T. Kuhns

For 2 People
1 c. water   1 c. Minute Rice   4 oz. Cheese Whiz

For 4 People
2 c. water   2 c. Minute Rice   8 oz. Cheese Whiz

Bring water to a boil. Add rice & cheese whiz. Cover & let set for 10 minutes. Stir after 5 minutes. Real easy & so good!

Cooked Dried Corn
Amish Acres Kitchen

2 c dried sweet corn	1 tsp salt
3 Tbsp butter	Warm water
2 tsp sugar	1/2 c cream or sweet milk

Soak corn for 1 hour in warm water that nearly covers the corn. Then cook corn until it is soft and the water is almost completely absorbed. Stir in salt, sugar, butter and cream or milk and bring to a boil. Serve.

Corn Casserole
Angie Pletcher-Stillson

1 can creamed style corn   1/2 c butter
1 can whole kernel corn (drained)   2 eggs
1 c sour cream (can substitute with plain yogurt)
1 box Jiffy corn muffin mix

Combine in 9x13 inch glass baking dish the corns, yogurt, softened butter and 3/4 Jiffy corn mix. Stir. Sprinkle remaining corn mix on top. Bake uncovered at 350 degrees for 30 to 35 minutes.

Corn Casserole
Bertha Hershberger

1 egg   1 c sour cream
1/2 c melted margarine   1 tsp sugar
1/2 tsp salt   1 can whole kernel corn
1 can cream style corn   1 pkg Jiffy corn muffin mix

Mix all ingredients and put in 2 qt greased dish. Use a "shallow dish" so center gets done. Bake at 350 degrees for 45 minutes.

Dill Tomatoes
Nicole Espey

1/2 c sour cream   1/4 c mayonnaise
2 Tbsp finely chopped onion   1/4 tsp dried dill weed
1/4 tsp salt

Sauce: Combine first five ingredients, mix well. Chill.

4 large tomatoes

Core tomatoes, cut in half crosswise. Season cut surface with salt and pepper, dot with butter. Broil cut side up 3 inches from heat for 5 min. Top with chilled sauce.

Dilly Beans
Mrs. Edwin Kuhns, granddaughter of M.T. Kuhns

2 lbs whole green beans
2 1/2 c water

2 1/2 c vinegar
1/4 c salt

In each pint jar put one clove garlic, 1/4 t. cayenne red pepper, 1 head dill. Boil water, vinegar and salt. Put in jars. Process 10 minutes in water bath. Good in 2 weeks. Fills 5 1/2 pints

Escarole Salad with Parmesan
Amish Acres Kitchen

3 cups torn escarole or curly endive
1/4 c chopped green onions
1/2 c whole kernel corn
2 tsp olive oil
1 Tbsp grated parmesan cheese

1/4 c chopped fresh parsley
1/4 c chopped green peppers
1/4 c lemon juice
Salt and black pepper to taste

In a large salad bowl, mix the escarole or endive, parsley, green onions, green peppers, red peppers, and corn. Add the lemon juice, olive oil, and Parmesan; toss well. Add salt and pepper to taste.

Garlic Dill Pickles
Mrs. Andrew Hochstetler, granddaughter of M.T. Kuhns

2 heads & 1 stalk dill
8 to 12 garlic buds
6 c sugar
4 Tbsp salt

Sliced pickles
2 c vinegar
6 c water

Combine dill, garlic and sliced pickles in 2 qt. Can. Mix together and boil rest of ingredients. Pour over pickles, dill, garlic buds. Cold pack to boiling. Remove immediately. Makes 7 to 8 qts.

61

Green Beans
Amish Acres Thresher Dinner

2 qts green beans, you may use fresh, frozen, or canned
2 tsp seasoned salt   1 1/2 tsp chopped onion
1/2 c diced ham

Drain green beans, add ingredients together and cook until hot.

Harvard Beets
Theme Buffet: Hello, Dolly! - *Chef Brenda Ritter*

3/4 c sugar   2 tsp cornstarch
1/3 c vinegar   1/3 c water
4 c cooked beets   3 Tbsp butter
1/4 tsp salt   1/8 tsp pepper

Combine sugar and cornstarch. Add vinegar and water.
Boil for 5 minutes. Add beets, simmer for 1/2 hour.

Hashbrown Casserole
Brenda Beehler

2 lbs frozen hashbrown cubes, thawed (or shredded hashbrowns)
1 can cream of chicken soup   8 oz sour cream
2 c shredded cheddar cheese   1 small onion, chopped
Garlic salt to taste   1 stick of butter
1 c seasoned crushed breadcrumbs

Mix together hashbrowns, soup, sour cream, cheese, onion and
garlic salt. Pour into 13x 9 inch pan. Cover and bake for 45 minutes. When bubbling uncover and sprinkle breadcrumbs and butter
over top. Bake for additional 10 to 15 minutes until brown.

Herbed Oven Potatoes
Andrea Stahly

1/2 c olive or vegetable oil
1 envelope onion soup mix
1 tsp dried marjoram
1/4 tsp pepper

1/4 c margarine, melted
1 tsp dried thyme
2 lbs red potatoes

In a shallow bowl, combine first 6 ingredients. Add a few potatoes at a time, toss to coat. Place in a single layer on a greased 15 x 10 x 1 pan. Drizzle remaining oil mixture over the potatoes. Bake uncovered at 450 degrees for 50 to 55 minutes or until tender.

Marinated Scallops
Theme Buffet: **Triumph of Love - *Chef Brenda Ritter***

1 lb scallops
2 bay leaves
1/4 tsp salt
1/2 c lemon juice
1 tsp tarragon

2 c water
2 cloves garlic
1/4 tsp celery salt
1/2 c olive oil
1 small onion

In an enamel saucepan combine all ingredients except scallops. Boil 15 to 20 minutes. Add scallops and cook until scallops are opaque. Serve hot or cold.

Mashed Potatoes
Shirley Pitney

8 to10 potatoes, peeled & mashed
8 oz cream cheese, cut in cubes

1 c sour cream
1 tsp garlic salt

Add to potatoes cream cheese, sour cream & garlic salt. Continue mashing potatoes and add milk (if needed) until potatoes have desired consistency. Place in buttered 2 quart casserole dish. Sprinkle top with paprika and dot with butter. Bake in 350 degree oven for 30 minutes (45 minutes if prepared night before and stored in refrigerator).

Mashed Potatoes
Amish Acres Thresher Dinner

6 large potatoes
1/4 c butter
Enough milk for consistency

1 to 2 t salt
3 oz cream cheese

Peel and dice potatoes. Boil in saucepan 10 to 15 minutes or until done. Drain. Add salt, butter, cream cheese, and milk. Whip until lumps are gone.

Melitzanosaltata
Theme Buffet: Zorba - Chef Brenda Ritter

1 large eggplant, peel & mash
1/2 c sour cream

1 tsp garlic powder
1 tsp parsley

Mix all ingredients, place in pan and bake for 30 minutes at 350 degrees.

Mohawk Corn
Theme Buffet: 1776 - Chef Brenda Ritter

4 c uncooked corn, freshly cut from cob
1/2 c shelled black walnuts

2 Tbsp butter
1/4 c maple sugar

Cook corn gently in a small amount of water until tender. Drain most of the liquid. Add butter, walnuts and maple sugar and stir until butter melts and sugar coats corn.

Parmesan Baked Potatoes
Laura Slabaugh

3 Tbsp grated parmesan cheese
8 medium unpeeled red potatoes, halved length wise

6 Tbsp oleo or butter

Pour butter into 9 x 13 inch pan. Sprinkle parmesan cheese over butter. Place potatoes with cut side down over cheese. Bake, uncovered at 400 degrees for 40 to 45 minutes.

New Potato Salad
Theme Buffet: Fiddler on the Roof - *Chef Brenda Ritter*

5 lbs new red potatoes (with skins)	3 c green onions, sliced thin
5 c celery, chopped	4 c mayonnaise
1/4 c dijon mustard	4 Tbsp vinegar
2 Tbsp sugar	1 tsp salt
2 tsp black pepper	2 Tbsp celery seed (whole)
10 hard boiled eggs (quartered lengthwise)	

Stem potatoes just until tender. Do not overcook.
Quarter potatoes, with skins on, lengthwise into wedges.
Combine all ingredients. Mix gently by hand to avoid
breaking up potatoes. Refrigerate.

Party Potatoes
Ruth Ann Miller

Part 1
10 medium potatoes (cook, let cool, peel & dice)

1 onion, chopped	1 green pepper, chopped
1/2 lb Velveeta cheese, diced	Salt & pepper to taste

Part 2

2 slices toast, cubed	1/2 c melted butter
1 1/2 c milk	

Part 3 Topping

1/4 c melted butter	1 1/2 c cornflake crumbs

Mix Part 1 and 2, put in baking dish. Mix topping and put on top.
Bake uncovered at 300 degrees for 45 minutes. Note: I use chopped
ham instead of the green pepper but you can use either or both.

Rice Pilaf
Theme Buffet: Zorba - Chef Brenda Ritter

2 oz butter
1 green pepper, chopped
1 c button mushrooms, chopped
1 c rice
1 tsp salt

1 red pepper, chopped
1 medium onion, chopped
1/2 oz chicken base
3 c water
1 tsp pepper

Saute' onion and peppers until tender in butter, add mushrooms.
Pour in water, add chicken base, salt and pepper. Bring to boil, add
rice, bring back to a boil and then turn off heat. Cover and let
stand until water is absorbed.

Rice Pilaf
Jenni Pletcher-Wysong

1/2 stick butter
1 can mushrooms
2 cans consomme'

1/2- 3/4 c. onion, diced
1 c white rice (uncooked)

Saute' mushrooms and onion until tender. Add consomme' and
rice. Bake uncovered for 1 hour at 350 degrees.

Root Vegetable Gratin
Amish Acres Kitchen

2 tsp butter
2 large turnips
2 cups heavy cream
1/2 cup Parmesan cheese or Gruyere cheese - grated

5 yukon gold potatoes
2 large yellow rutabaga
4 sage leaves

Clean, peel, and slice all root vegetables. Preheat oven to 375
degrees. Butter a gratin dish and arrange layers of potatoes, then
turnips, and rutabagas. Season between each layer with salt and
pepper, continuing to you reach the top of the dish. Heat the
cream with the sage leaves, and pour over vegetables. Cover with
grated cheese and bake for 40 to 50 minutes, until vegetables are
softened. Test with a skewer for doneness.

Scalloped Dried Corn
Amish Acres Kitchen

3 c crushed soda crackers
1 can dried corn
3 Tbsp butter

1/8 tsp pepper
1 Tbsp salt
2 c milk

Into a 2 qt buttered casserole dish put 1 c crushed crackers.
Sprinkle with 1/2 tsp salt and a dash of pepper. Dot with 1 Tbsp
butter. Cover with half of corn and another cup of crackers.
Pour milk over the whole and dot with remaining butter.
Cover casserole and bake at 375 degrees for 35 minutes.
Uncover and brown 10 minutes.

Seven Bean Salad
Theme Buffet: Fiddler on the Roof - Chef Brenda Ritter

1 can garbanzo beans
1 can green beans
1 cup lima beans
1 cup pinto beans
2 scallions, chopped thinly
2 cups honey or corn syrup

1 can kidney beans
1 can yellow/wax beans
1 cup white northern beans
1 medium onion sliced very thin
2 cups cider vinegar

Drain and rinse all beans. Combine onions and scallions.
Blend vinegar and honey thoroughly and pour over vegetables.
Refrigerate at least 4 hours.

Southern Style Hash Browns
Kathy Hockert

2 lbs southern style hash browns
1 - 16 oz sour cream
8 oz grated cheddar cheese

1 can cream chicken
1 Tbsp butter, melted

Mix all ingredients and bake at 350 degrees for 1 hour.

Spanish Rice
Theme Buffet: Meet Me in St. Louis - *Chef Brenda Ritter*

1 Tbsp vegetable oil
1/4 onion, chopped
Salt and pepper to taste
4 c water

2 c long grain white rice
1 green bell pepper, chopped
1 - 14.5oz can stewed tomatoes

In large skillet combine oil, rice, onion, green pepper and salt and pepper until rice is a light brown color. Remove from stove. Mix tomatoes into mixture. Pour in water covering entire mixture. Return the skillet to stovetop and bring to a full boil. Add salt and pepper to taste. When mixture begins to boil, cover skillet and reduce heat to simmer. Cook 12 to15 minutes without removing cover. Turn off stove and let stand for 12 to 15 minutes without removing cover until time is up.

Stuffed Green Peppers
Susan Nunemaker

4 large green peppers, (washed & cored reserve tops)
1 lb ground beef
Chopped onions

4 Tbsp tomato sauce
Salt & pepper to taste

Fry beef until done. Put in colander & rinse with hot water. Wipe excess grease from pan. Add beef & stir in tomato sauce & onions. Heat thoroughly. Stuff into peppers. Place in baking dish & add 2 cups water. Cover & bake in at 350 degrees oven for 1/2 hour. Check water frequently. Pour out water & bake additional 15 minutes.

Stuffing with Apples & Raisins
Theme Buffet: Annie Get Your Gun - *Chef Brenda Ritter*

1 qt hot water
1 tsp pepper
1 1/2 c celery, chopped
5 eggs beaten slightly
1 1/2 c salad oil
1/4 c chicken base

1 tsp poultry seasoning
1 tsp seasoning salt
1 1/2 c onion, chopped
1 c chopped apples
1 c raisins
2 loaves stale bread, in pieces

Mix first nine ingredients, add bread pieces then raisins and apples. Mix until moist. Bake at 350 degrees for 1 hour covered, then uncover and brown.

Sweet Potato Casserole
Verda Hochstetler

3 c sweet potatoes (cooked & mashed)
2 eggs (beaten)
1/2 c margarine (melted)

1 c sugar
1 c milk
1 tsp vanilla

Topping:
1/2 c brown sugar
2 Tbsp margarine

1/4 c chopped pecans

Mix together and stir well - sweet potatoes, sugar, eggs, milk, margarine and vanilla. Put in 2 qt. Greased casserole dish and add topping. Cover and bake in 350 oven for 1 hour. Dot with miniature marshmallows last 5 minutes (optional).

Zucchini Casserole
Bertha Hershberger

3 c shredded zucchini
1/2 c vegetable oil
1/2 tsp garlic salt
1/2 c mozzarella cheese

4 beaten eggs
1/3 c chopped onion
1 Tbsp parsley
1 c dry bisquick

Mix all ingredients together. Pour into greased casserole pan. Bake at 350 degrees for 25 to 30 minutes.

Tandoori Potato Wedges
Theme Buffet: **Brigadoon** - *Chef Brenda Ritter*

2 medium potatoes washed and scrubbed
2 Tbsp tandoori paste

Cut each potato into 8 equal wedges. Brush each wedge with a light coating of tandoori paste and place them on their backs in a microwave dish. Cover with film and pierce the center. Cook in the microwave on high for 6 minutes. For firmer wedges bake at 375 degrees for 30 to 35 minutes. Serve with dips. Makes an ideal appetizer.

Tator Tot Casserole
Jacob and Loretta Kuhns, great-grandson of M.T. Kuhns

4 lbs hamburger, fried in onions
2 cans cream of mushroom soup
4 lbs frozen vegetables
Velveeta cheese

1 pkg taco seasoning
1 can milk
2 bags frozen tator tots

Fry hamburger with onions & seasoning. Mix in mushroom soup & soup can milk. Put in large roaster - layer with vegetables & tator tots. Put cheese on top and bake 1 3/4 hours at 350 degrees.

Three Bean Casserole
Verda Hochstetler

1 pkg frozen lima beans (10 oz)
1 can kidney beans (16 oz)
1 small onion (cut up)
2 Tbsp chili sauce
1/4 tsp dry mustard

1 can baked beans (16 oz)
1 can tomato sauce (8 oz)
1 Tbsp brown sugar
1 tsp salt

Pour into 1 1/2 qt casserole dish. Arrange Spam slices in spoke fashion to top. Bake at 400 degrees for 30 minutes.

Zucchini Casserole
Brenda Beehler

2 large zucchini squash
1/2 tsp garlic salt
1/4 tsp pepper
3 eggs, beaten
1 c buttered dried breadcrumbs

2 med onions, chopped
1 tsp oregano
1 c cheddar cheese, shredded
1 lb bulk sausage

Peel zucchini, cube and cook in boiling water for 20 minutes.
Drain zucchini and mash slightly, leaving some chunks.
Brown sausage and onion, mix with zucchini, seasonings, eggs and
cheese. Put in casserole pan and top with breadcrumbs. Bake at 375
degrees for 30 to 45 minutes.

Zucchini Fritters
Irene O. Miller

2 Tbsp onion, chopped
1 egg
1 c zucchini, shredded
1/8 tsp garlic salt
1/8 tsp accent

1/2 c flour
1 carrot shredded
1/8 tsp onion salt
1/4 tsp Lawry's Seasoned Salt

Fry in patties & top with a slice of cheese.
Good with tomato or hamburger.

Main Dishes

Arkansas Razor Back Ham
Theme Buffet: Big River - *Chef Brenda Ritter*

1 - 5 lb sugar cured ham	1 c brown sugar
1 c honey	1/4 c powdered mustard

Score ham. Baste with mixture of sugar, honey and mustard every 1/2 hour. Bake for 1 1/2 hours.

Baked Breakfast Burritos
Laura Slabaugh

6 or 8 bacon strips	8 fresh mushrooms, sliced
6 green onions, sliced	1/3 c green peppers, chopped
1 garlic clove, minced	8 eggs
3 Tbsp enchilada or taco sauce	1/4 c sour cream
3/4 c shredded cheese cheddar or co jack	
1 Tbsp oleo or butter	4 large flour tortillas - 9 inch
Sour cream and additional sauce	

In a skillet cook bacon till crisp. Drain. Reserve 1 Tbsp drippings. Sauté mushrooms, onions, green peppers, and garlic in dripping until tender. Set aside and keep warm. In a bowl beat eggs and sour cream. Stir in 1/4 c cheese and sauce. In a skillet melt butter and add egg mixture. Cook over low heat till eggs are set. Remove from heat. Crumble bacon and add to eggs with mushroom mixture. Spoon down center of tortillas. Roll up and place seam down in a 11 x 7 inch baking dish. Sprinkle with remaining cheese. Bake at 350 degrees for 5 minutes or till cheese melts. Serve with sour cream and sauce.

Barbecue Chicken
Wanda Kuhns

6 c corn flakes or rice krispie crumbs	
1 tsp pepper	1 tsp seasoned salt
2 tsp dry mustard	

Mix all together. Melt butter dip chicken pieces in butter then in crumbs but on cookie sheets & bake 1 hour. Then put in roaster for 1/2 hour.

Baked Pizza Sandwich
Mrs. Wilbur Kuhns, great-grandson of M.T. Kuhns

1 lb hamburger
1 tsp oregano
1/4 c parmesan cheese
1 c milk
1 can cream of mushroom soup

1 pint pizza sauce
1 - 8 oz cream cheese
2 c Bisquick
1 egg

Fry & drain meat. Stir half of pizza sauce & the oregano into meat. Bring to a boil. Reduce heat & simmer for 10 minutes. Mix the bisquick, egg, & milk. Measure 3/4 of batter into greased pan. Pour remaining sauce over batter; spread evenly. Layer slices of cream cheese , meat mixture, mushroom soup, remaining cheese slices, & batter on top. Bake uncovered at 400 degrees until brown, 20 to 25 minutes.

Barbecue Beef
Gloria Fimbianti

2 lbs ground beef
1 green pepper
1 tsp salt
2 Tbsp mustard
3/4 c catsup

1 onion, chopped
Celery, chopped
1 tsp sugar
1 Tbsp vinegar
1 small can tomato sauce

Combine salt, sugar catsup, tomato sauce, vinegar.
Simmer 20 minutes. Sauté onion and ground beef. Add celery and green pepper. Combine with tomato mixture. Simmer 30 minutes. Add mustard last. Heat through.

Beef
Amish Acres Thresher Dinner

5 lbs chuck roast
3 Tbsp beef base

2 Tbsp meat tenderizer

Cut Roast in sliced 3" cubes. Put roast in casserole dish. Add meat tenderizer and beef base on meat. Fill with water and cook at 300 degrees for 4 to 5 hours.

BBQ Beef Patties
Sharon Slabaugh, great-granddaughter of M.T. Kuhns

1 c bread or cracker crumbs	1/2 c milk
1 lb hamburger	1 tsp salt
1/4 tsp pepper	3 Tbsp brown sugar
1 1/2 Tbsp Worcestershire sauce	1/2 c ketchup
1/2 tsp salt	1/2 c onions

Moisten crumbs with milk. Combine with meat, salt and pepper. Shape into 6 patties onto jelly roll pan. Combine remaining ingredients to make BBQ topping. Spoon over hamburgers. Bake at 350 degrees for 30 to 40 minutes.

Beef and Noodles
Amish Acres Thresher Dinner

2 lbs cooked noodles	16 oz canned chunk beef
2 pts beef broth	2 pts water
1 to 2 tsp black pepper	

Mix beef, broth, water, pepper in a pan and bring to a boil. Add noodles, turn down heat to simmer and cook for 20 to 30 minutes.

Breakfast Pizza
Mary E. Miller, granddaughter of M.T. Kuhns

1 lb pork sausage	1 pkgs crescent rolls
1 c hash browns	1 c shredded cheddar cheese
5 eggs	1/4 c milk
1/2 tsp salt	Pepper to taste

Cook sausage until brown, drain fat. Separate rolls and place on round 12 inch pan with points to center. Press sides to form crust. Sprinkle with potatoes, sausage and cheddar cheese. Mix eggs, milk, salt and pepper. Pour over all. Bake at 375 degrees for 25 to 30 minutes.

Beef Burgundy
Theme Buffet: Meet Me in St. Louis - *Chef Brenda Ritter*

5 lbs lean stewing beef (remove gristle)
Salt & pepper
3/4 lb smoked bacon, diced
3 large carrots, coarsely chopped
6 medium onions, coarsely chopped
2 tsp thyme
3/4 c flour
Lemon juice
1 lb mushrooms, small
Parsley

Flour (to dredge meat)
Butter & oil (to brown meat)
3 to 4 cloves garlic, minced
1 c chopped parsley
3 bay leaves
1 bottle Burgundy wine
1/3 lb butter
1/4 c butter
1 lb baby onions

Cut meat into 1 1/2 inch cubes. Toss in flour, salt and pepper mixture. Brown in small batches in half butter and half oil. Remove to Dutch oven or deep casserole dish. Fry bacon until crisp, add to beef. In bacon fat, brown the garlic, carrots and onions. Add vegetables to beef and cover with wine (add water if needed to cover completely.) Bake about an hour at 350 degrees. Make a paste with butter and flour and stir this in well. Add a dash of lemon juice. Continue to bake until meat is tender (about 2 hours). Lightly brown baby onions in 2 t butter, add a little water to cover and simmer then until cooked. Just before serving melt 2 T. butter and sauté mushrooms briefly over high heat. **To serve:** Spread about half of onions and mushrooms over top of beef, sprinkle with chopped parsley. Pass separate warmed bowls of extra mushrooms and onion for topping.

Campbell's Beef Taco Bake
Jeff and Angie Stillson

1 lb ground beef
1 can condensed tomato soup
6 flour tortillas cut into 1" pieces

1 cup salsa
1/2 c milk
1 c shredded cheddar cheese

Brown ground beef, add soup, salsa, milk, tortillas and 1/2 of the cheese. Spoon in baking dish. Cover. Bake at 400 degrees for 30 minutes. Add remaining cheese.

Beef Wellington
Theme Buffet: **Brigadoon -** *Chef Brenda Ritter*

3 lbs fillet or beef
1 1/2 oz butter
8 oz sliced button mushrooms
1 egg beaten, to glaze

1 Tbsp oil
6 oz smooth liver pate'
12 oz puff pastry

Trim and tie up the fillet at intervals with fine string so it retains its shape. Heat the oil and 1/2 oz. Butter in large frying pan, add meat and fry briskly on all sides. Press down with wooden spoon while frying to seal well. Roast 20 minutes. then set the beef aside to cool and remove string. Meanwhile, cook the mushrooms in remaining butter until soft, leave until cold, then blend with the pate. On lightly floured surface, roll out the pastry into a large rectangle, about 13x11 inches and 1/4 inch thick. Spread the pate mixture down the center of the pastry. Place meat down center on top. Brush the edges of pastry with the egg. Fold the pastry edges over lengthways and turn the parcel over so that the joint is underneath. Fold the ends under the meat on the baking sheet. Decorate with leaves cut from the pastry trimmings. Brush with remaining egg and bake for 50 to 60 minutes at 425 degrees.
Let stand for 10 minutes before serving.

Big Jim's Trotline Catfish
Theme Buffet: **Big River -** *Chef Brenda Ritter*

4 catfish fillets
Pepper, as needed

Garlic salt, as needed
Cayenne pepper if desired

Sprinkle fillets with seasoning as desired. Place fillets in oiled fish basket or on oiled grill. Grill 4 to 5 minutes per side or until fish is done. Top with Mango Salsa.

Mango Salsa
1 whole mango, peeled, seeded and diced
1 whole papaya, peeled, seeded and diced
1 Tbsp chopped red jalapeno pepper
2 Tbsp freshly squeezed lime juice
1 Tbsp chopped green onion
1 Tbsp honey

Stir all ingredients in bowl. Let salsa stand at room temp for 15 to 20 minutes before serving. Using slotted spoon, serve over grilled catfish.

Breakfast Burritos
Ruth Ann Miller

1 bag (16 oz) frozen southern-style hash browns
12 eggs
1 large onion, chopped
1 green pepper, chopped
1/2 pound bulk sausage, browned and drained
12 flour tortillas (10 inch), warmed
3 cups (12 oz) shredded cheddar cheese
Salsa optional

In a large skillet, fry hash browns according to package directions; remove and set aside. In a large bowl, beat eggs; add onions and green pepper. Pour into the same skillet; cook and stir until eggs are set. Remove from heat. Add hash browns and sausage; mix gently. Place about 3/4 cup of filling on each tortilla and top with about 1/4 c cheese. Roll up and place on a greased baking sheet. Bake at 350 degrees for 15 to 20 minutes or until heated through. Serve with salsa if desired.

Breakfast Casserole
Kathryn Mishler, great-granddaughter of M.T. Kuhns

12 piece of bread
3 c milk
Salt & pepper to taste
16 oz cheddar cheese

6 eggs
2 1/2 c ham cubes
16 oz mozzarella cheese

Grease pan. Put 6 pieces of bread in bottom of pan. Mix eggs, milk, ham and salt & pepper and put 1/2 of the mixture on top of the bread. Repeat layers with remaining bread and mixture. Sprinkle cheeses on top. Refrigerate overnight. Before putting in oven, top with 3 c cornflakes and 1/2 c butter. Bake for 45 to 60 minutes.

Breakfast Casserole
Carolyn Hershberger, great-granddaughter of M.T. Kuhns

2 c flour
1/3 c oil
3/4 c milk

2 Tbsp baking powder
Pinch of salt

2 or 3 medium potatoes
1 can cream of mushroom soup
1/2 lb bacon (cut up)
1/2 stick butter

1/2 can milk or water
14 eggs
9 slices cheese

Mix first 5 ingredients for crust. Press in 9x13 inch cake pan & bake at 350 degrees for 10 to 15 minutes. Shred potatoes & fry until tender. Layer on baked crust. Mix soup & milk or water & pour over potatoes. Scramble eggs, fry bacon, & layer eggs, bacon, cheese & corn flakes crumbs mixed with 1/2 stick of butter on top.
Bake again for 20 minutes.

Brenda's Prime Rib
Theme Buffet: **Fiddler on the Roof -** *Chef Brenda Ritter*

4 lb Rib Roast
6 Tbsp freshed chopped garlic

1/2 c salt
2 Tbsp pepper

The night before, rub roast with salt, pepper, and garlic. Cover and refrigerate overnight. Roast in oven for 20 to 25 minutes at 450 degrees, until well browned. Lower oven temp tp 350 degrees and finish roasting until desired doneness, usually 1 1/2 to 2 hours.

Chicken Cordon Bleu Casserole
Anna Marie Schmucker

5 chicken breasts (skinless, chunks)
4 eggs, beaten
1/4 lb Swiss cheese

2 c cracker crumbs
1/4 lb ham

Dip chicken pieces in eggs then roll in cracker crumbs. Brown in oil. Put in oblong pan and top with ham and cheese.
Sauce mix: 1/2 c. sour cream, 1 can cream of mushroom soup. Pour over top and bake at 375 degrees for 30 to 45 minutes.

Burrito Casserole

Norma O. Kuhns, great-granddaughter of M.T. Kuhns

2 lbs hamburger
1 can refried beans
2 cans cream of mushroom soup

1 pkg taco seasoning
1 box sour cream
Tortillas

Brown hamburger. Add taco seasoning & beans. Mix sour cream & mushroom soup together; set aside. Line bottom of pan with tortillas. Put half of sour cream mixture, next add meat. Cover with tortillas, the add rest of sour cream mixture over tortillas. Put cheese on top. Bake for 1 hour at 325 degrees. Top with lettuce, tomatoes, & salsa.

Burritos

Jenni Pletcher-Wysong

3 c shredded cheddar cheese
1 c picante (divided)
1/2 c sliced green onion
8 to 10 flour tortillas
Chopped lettuce
1 c ground beef, browned & strained

3 oz cream cheese
1 medium red pepper
1 tsp cumin
1 tomato, chopped
1 can refried beans

Combine 2 cups cheese, cream cheese, 1/4 cup picante, red pepper, onion, and cumin. Mix in ground beef and refried beans. Add tomato and lettuce. Spoon 1/4 cup of the mixture in each tortilla, roll and place seam side down in a greased 9 x 13 inch pan. Pour remainder of picante over top and sprinkle with cheese. Cover and bake at 350 degrees for 20 minutes.

Chicken & Dumplings
Ruth Ann Miller

2 lbs chicken, cooked & shredded	1/2 tsp salt
1 - 14 oz chicken broth	1 can cream of celery soup
1 1/4 c water or cream	1/4 c butter
1 egg	3/4 c milk or cream
1 1/2 c flour	1 1/4 tsp baking powder

In 5 qt saucepan over medium heat, stir soup, cooked chicken, water, and butter until smooth. Bring to a boil. Reduce heat to low and simmer. Meanwhile, in a liquid measuring cup, beat egg. Add enough cream to measure 1 cup. Combine flour, baking powder, parsley and salt. Stir in egg mixture just until flour is moistened (dough will be soft and sticky). Drop dough into simmering liquid. Cover and let simmer for 10 minutes.

Chicken Divan
Susie Pletcher

2 - 10 oz frozen broccoli, cooked and drained

2 c sliced cooked chicken breasts	2 c cream of chicken soup
1 c light mayonnaise	1 tsp lemon juice
1/2 tsp curry powder	1/2 c shredded cheese
1/2 c soft bread crumbs	1 Tbsp melted butter

Arrange broccoli in 9x13 inch pan. Place chicken on top. Combine soup, juice, mayo, curry powder and pour over chicken. Sprinkle cheese on top. Combine crumbs and butter and place on top. Bake at 350 degrees for 45 minutes.

Chicken Flour (for Broasted/Fried Chicken)
Amish Acres Threshers Dinner

2 c flour	1/2 c seasoned salt
1 Tbsp garlic salt	1 Tbsp black pepper
2 Tbsp meat tenderizer	1/2 c ground mustard

Mix all together. Place mixture in bag. Put chicken in bag and shake well. Cook to your preference.

Chicken Fried Rice
Nicole Espey

1/2 c sliced green onions
1/4 c chopped red bell pepper
1/2 tsp crushed red pepper flakes
6 tsp egg beaters
2 Tbsp soy sauce

1/4 c sliced celery
1 clove garlic, crushed
2 tsp peanut oil
2 c cooked diced chicken
1 tsp sugar

3 c cooked regular long grain rice, prepared in unsalted water

In large non-stick skillet over high heat, sauté onions, celery, pepper, garlic in oil until tender-crisp. Pour egg beaters into skillet, cook, stirring occasionally until mixture is set. Stir in rice, chicken, soy sauce and sugar, cook until heated through.

Chicken Fried Steak
Theme Buffet: Fiddler on the Roof - *Chef Brenda Ritter*

6 beef cube steaks
4 c flour
1/4 c garlic salt
1/4 c seasoning salt

1 qt buttermilk
1/2 c powdered mustard
2 tsp black pepper
1 tsp poultry seasoning

Soak steak in buttermilk for at least 4 hours. Drain and combine all dry ingredients. Flour steak, fry in oil until brown and crispy.

Chicken Rice Casserole
Bertha Hershberger

1/2 c onion
1 c chopped celery
1 c slightly cooked rice
2 c chicken broth
2 cans cream of chicken soup

1/4 c margarine
2 c cooked chicken
1/2 tsp salt
1 tsp curry powder

Sauté onions and butter until onions are tender. Mix all other ingredients together. Place in 9 x 13 inch pan. Bake at 350 degrees for 1 1/2 hours.

Chicken Leek & Field Mushroom Pie
Theme Buffet: **My Fair Lady** - *Chef Brenda Ritter*

2 - 9 x 11 sheets for puff pastry
Filling:
1 qt large cooked white meat chicken, diced
1/2 c chopped leeks   1 c sliced mushrooms
2 c heavy cream   1 Tbsp chicken base
2 c hot water   1/2 tsp white pepper
4 oz butter, melted   1/2 c flour

Spray 9x11 inch pan with cooking spray, line pan with sheet of puff pastry. Prick with fork tines every inch or so. Bake 10 minutes at 400 degrees. Remove from oven to cool.

Filling: Combine water, chicken base and pepper, bring to a boil. Reduce heat and simmer for 10 minutes. Add chicken and simmer 15 minutes more. Increase heat and add heavy cream, leeks and mushrooms, bring to almost a boil. Add flour, stirring constantly cook for 10 minutes. Pour into pan lined with puff pastry. Prick with fork. Bake at 400 degrees for 30 minutes or until golden.

Chicken Pot Pie
Ruth Ann Miller

2 1/2 c flour   1 c milk
4 c chicken broth, hot   2 c chicken, cooked & diced
1 c peas, cooked   1 c carrots, cooked
Pepper   Celery salt
3/4 c shortening   3/4 c salt
1 egg, separated   1/2 c hot water

Blend half of the flour with the milk, stir into hot broth and cook until thick and smooth. Add the chicken, peas, carrots, pepper and celery salt. Pour mixture into buttered casserole or dish.

Dough:
Cut in the shortening into remaining flour with the salt. Stir in the beaten egg yolk, blended with water and form a soft dough. Roll to 1/2 inch thickness, cut to fit top of baking dish. Pierce opening for steam to escape. Brush with egg white. Bake at 350 degrees for 35 minutes.

Chicken over Spanish Rice
Theme Buffet: **Man of La Mancha** - *Chef Brenda Ritter*

2 tsp olive oil
4 oz long grain white rice — 1/2 c chopped onion
1 1/2 c canned crushed tomatoes — 1/4 c chopped fresh parsley
Coarsely ground black pepper — 1 c thawed frozen peas
4 skinned and boned chicken breasts (3 oz. each)
1 c chopped jarred roasted red pepper
1 tsp chopped fresh rosemary or 1/4 t. rosemary leaves
1 c canned ready-to-serve low sodium chicken broth
Rosemary sprigs and lemon wedges for garnish

In 12 inch nonstick skillet, heat oil. Add chicken and cook, turning once until browned, 5 to 7 minutes. Transfer chicken to a plate, set aside. In same skillet combine rice and onion. Cook until rice is translucent, about 2 minutes. Stir in tomatoes, roasted red pepper, broth, parsley, rosemary and salt. Return chicken to skillet, cover and let simmer for 25 minutes. Stir in peas and cook until rice is tender, about 5 minutes. To serve, arrange chicken-rice mixture on serving platter, sprinkle with ground pepper to taste and garnish with rosemary sprigs and lemon wedges.

Crock Pot Pizza
Sandy Stavedahl

1 lb hamburger — 1 pkg sliced pepperoni
1/2 green pepper, diced — 1 onion, chopped
2 cans Chef-boy Ardee pizza sauce — 2 c shredded cheddar cheese
2 c shredded pizza cheese
1 box rigattoni noodles, (cooked & drained)

Layer in crock pot: 1 can pizza sauce, 1/2 hamburger,
1/2 pepperoni, 1/2 onion, 1/2 green pepper, 1/2 cooked noodles,
1 cup chedder cheese and 1 cup pizza cheese. Then repeat 1 can pizza sauce, 1/2 hamburger, 1/2 pepperoni, 1/2 onion, 1/2 green pepper, 1/2 cooked noodles, and finish with remaining cheeses.
Heat on high for 3 to 4 hours or until cheese is melted.

Dried Beef Casserole
Frieda Miller

1 pkg dried beef	1 c macaroni (uncooked)
2 hard boiled eggs	1 c milk
1 can cream of mushroom soup	1/4 lb Velveeta cheese
Salt to taste	

Mix all together, put into 1 1/2 to 2 qt casserole dish and refrigerate over night. Bake uncovered at 350 degrees for 30 minutes or until bubbly.

Dublin Coddle
Shirley Pitney

1 1/2 lb pork sausage links	8 thick slices bacon
2 lbs potatoes, thinly sliced	3 large onions, thinly sliced
1 Tbsp salt	1/2 tsp pepper
1/4 c chopped parsley	

In 12" skillet over medium heat, brown sausage & bacon. Add 3 cups hot water & bring to boil. Cover & simmer for 10 minutes. Preheat oven to 350 degrees. Transfer sausages & bacon to 3 1/2 qt casserole, reserving liquid. Top meat with layers of potatoes, onions, parsley, salt and pepper. Cover all with liqued and bake 75 minutes or until potatoes are fork tender. Serves 8.

Easy Stroganoff
Gloria Fimbianti

1 1/2 lb sirloin, cut into strips	2 Tbsp butter
1 - 4 oz can mushrooms, drained	2 Tbsp flour
1 envelope dry onion soup mix	1 c milk
1 c water	1/2 c sour cream
2 Tbsp sherry	

Brown steak in butter. Add mushrooms. Stir in onion soup mix and flour. Add milk and water. Cook, stirring constantly, till slightly thickened. Cook over low heat for 45 minutes. Stir twice while cooking. Blend in cream and sherry. Heat through. Do not boil. Serve over rice or noodles.

Egg and Sausage Strata
Ruth Ann Miller

12 slices white bread, crusts removed, cubed
1 jar (2 ounces) chopped pimientos, drained
1 1/2 pounds bulk pork sausage   1/3 c chopped onion
1/4 c chopped green pepper   6 eggs
3 c milk   2 tsp Worcestershire sauce
1 tsp dry mustard   1/2 tsp salt
1/4 tsp pepper   1/4 tsp dried oregano

Line a greased 13x9x2 inch pan with bread cubes; set aside. In a skillet, brown sausage with the onion and green pepper; drain. Stir in pimientos; sprinkle over bread. In a bowl, beat eggs, milk, Worcestershire sauce, mustard, salt, pepper and oregano. Pour over sausage mixture. Cover and refrigerate overnight. Bake, covered, at 325 degrees for 1 hour and 20 minutes. Uncover and bake 10 minutes longer or until a knife inserted near the center comes out clean. Let stand 10 minutes before serving.

Deep Dish Taco Squares
Manass and Mary Lou Kuhns, great-grandson of M.T. Kuhns

1/2 lb ground beef   1/2 c sour cream
1/2 c shredded cheese   1 to 2 tomatoes, sliced
1/3 c mayonnaise or salad dressing   1/2 c onions, chopped
1/2 c green peppers, chopped   1 c Bisquick
1/2 c cold water

Heat oven to 375 degrees. Grease an 8x8 inch pan.
Brown ground beef and drain. Mix sour cream, cheese,
& mayonnaise, set aside. Mix Bisquick and water until soft dough forms. Put dough into pan, pressing it 1/2 inch up the sides of the pan. Layer beef, tomatoes, peppers, & onions on dough. Spoon and spread sour cream mixture on top. Bake at 350 degrees for 25 to 30 minutes or until edges are brown.

Egg Casserole
Delores Kauffman, great-granddaughter of M.T. Kuhns

2 lbs sausage, browned (may use ham or bacon)
24 oz hash browns, thawed
2 c cheddar cheese
8 eggs
1/2 tsp seasoned salt

1/2 c melted butter
2 c mozzarella cheese
1 c milk

Put hash browns in bottom of greased 9x13 inch pan. Drizzle with melted butter. Bake at 425 degrees for 25 minutes. Layer meat & cheese over potatoes. Beat eggs, milk, & seasoned salt together. Pour over top. Bake 40 more minutes at 350 degrees.

Enchilada Casserole
Jenni Pletcher-Wysong

2 c cooked chicken, cubed
1 c chicken broth or bouillon
1 can cream of chicken soup
1 can (4 oz) chopped green chilies
12 taco shells quartered or taco chips

1 c monterey jack cheese
1 c grated cheddar cheese
1 small onion, chopped
1 clove garlic, crushed

Mix chicken, broth, soup, green chilies, onion, garlic. In a greased 1 1/2 quart baking dish, layer 1/2 taco shells or chips and 1/2 chicken mixture. Repeat layers. Top with cheese. Bake at 375 degrees for 25 to 30 minutes.

Grilled Salmon Brushed with Butter
Theme Buffet: Smoke on the Mountain - *Chef Brenda Ritter*

1 bunch of chives
1/2 c lemon juice

1 bunch of parsley
1 c olive oil

Mix chives, parsley, lemon juice, and olive oil.
Coat salmon with mixture and serve.

Glazed Ham Patties
Susan Nunemaker

1 egg
1 c soft bread crumbs
2 Tbsp onions, grated
1/4 tsp salt
1 c sour cream

1/3 c milk
3 Tbsp chopped parsley
2 tsp prepared mustard
1 lb ground ham

In a large bowl beat together eggs & milk. Stir in crumbs, parsley, onions, mustard & salt. Mix lightly in ham until blended. Shape into 6 patties. Place on broiler pan & broil 3 to 4 inches from heat for about 10 minutes. Turn & broil 5 to 7 more minutes. Turn off. Spoon sour cream over patties. Leave in broiler 3 to 5 minutes to heat & glaze the sour cream.

Greek Chicken
Theme Buffet: Zorba - *Chef Brenda Ritter*

2 whole chickens cut in pieces
1/3 c salt
1/2 c cider vinegar
2 1/2 Tbsp Worcestershire sauce
1/2 c soy sauce

6 c water
1/4 c brown sugar
1 stick butter
2 Tbsp garlic powder

Boil sauce 15 minutes. Add chicken and simmer for additional 15 minutes. Remove chicken, place in a baking pan. Add 1 c sauce. Sprinkle with tarragon leaves. Bake 25 minutes or until brown.

Green Bean-Hamburger Casserole
Verda Hochstetler

1 lb hamburger
1 qt green beans
1 can cream of mushroom soup

2 medium onions (cut-up)
1 c milk
1 pkg tator tots

Brown hamburger and onion in a large skillet. Place in baking dish. Add green beans. Mix cream of mushroom soup and milk and pour over beans and hamburger. Top with tator tots. Bake at 350 degrees for 1 hour.

Ham
Amish Acres Thresher Dinner

3 lb ham, sliced
2 Tbsp brown sugar
1 small onion diced or sliced

1/2 c cider
1 Tbsp whole cloves

Mix all ingredients together and drizzle across ham.
Cook ham at 300 degrees for 30 to 45 minutes or until hot.

Hamburger Potato Casserole
Mrs. Nathan Miller, great-granddaughter of M.T. Kuhns

1 1/2 lb hamburger, browned & drained
8 medium potatoes, boiled, peeled & shredded
1/2 pkg taco seasoning
2 c grated cheese
1 small onion, chopped
1 can cream of mushroom soup
2 1/2 c cornflakes, crushed

1/4 c butter, melted
1 tsp salt
1 pint sour cream
1 can milk

Put hamburger in a greased cake pan. Combine all the other ingredients except cornflakes. Pour potato mixture over hamburger.
Mix together cornflakes with 1/4 c. butter. Spread crumbs on top of potatoes. Bake at 350 degrees for 45 minutes. May be prepared & refrigerated till ready to use.

Low Fat Chicken Rice
Nancy Hamman

1 c cream of chicken soup
3/4 c rice
4 chicken breasts

1 1/2 c water
Salt - pepper

Mix and pour in 9x13 inch pan. Place 4 chicken breasts on top and cover with foil. Bake at 375 degrees until chicken is done.

Husband's Delight
Laura Kuhns, great-granddaughter of M.T. Kuhns

1 lb hamburger
1 tsp salt
1 Tbsp sugar
1 tsp pepper
4 oz cream cheese
1 - 8 oz pkg noodles

2 cans tomato or pizza sauce
1/4 tsp garlic salt
1 Tbsp Worcestershire sauce
8 oz sour cream
1 onion, chopped

Brown hamburger and drain. Add tomato sauce and seasonings.
Simmer for 15 minutes. Blend in sour cream and cream cheese,
add onion. Cook noodles and drain. Place a layer of noodles in a
greased baking dish. Cover with a layer of meat mixture.
Top with cream cheese mixture. Repeat layers. Bake at 350 degrees
for 30 minutes.

Italian Lasagna
Theme Buffet: Meet Me in St. Louis - *Chef Brenda Ritter*

9 thick slices bacon, diced
1 tsp fennel seed
1 1/2 tsp Italian seasoning
2 lbs Italian sausage
1 - 16 oz pkg dry lasagna noodles
2 pints part-skim ricotta cheese
1/3 c milk
6 c shredded mozzarella cheese

1 onion, chopped
1 tsp dried oregano
2 - 29 oz cans tomato sauce
2 eggs
1 tsp dried oregano
2 tsp chopped fresh parsley
8 slices provolone cheese

Brown bacon and onion in a large pan over medium heat. Stir in
fennel seed, 1 t oregano, Italian seasoning and tomato sauce. Cover
and simmer on low for 4 to 6 hours, or until thick. Brown sausage
links in large skillet. Drain on paper towels, cut into 1 inch pieces.
Mix together ricotta cheese, egg, milk, parsley, 1 t oregano in a
medium bowl. Layer 1 cup of sauce on the bottom of a 9x13 inch
pan. Layer with 1/3 uncooked lasagna noodles, 1/2 ricotta cheese
mixture, 1/2 sausage pieces, 1/3 mozzarella and 1/2 provolone
cheese. Top with 1/3 sauce. Repeat layers. Top with remaining 1/3
noodles and spread with remaining sauce. Sprinkle with 1/3 mozzarella cheese. Bake at 350 degrees for 1 1/2 hours.

Maryland Crab Cakes
Andrea Stahly

1 egg	1/4 c milk
3 Tbsp mayonnaise	1 Tbsp all purpose flour
1 Tbsp Worcestershire sauce	1 tsp mustard
1 tsp salt	1/4 tsp pepper
1/2 c dry bread crumbs	2 Tbsp margarine

1 lb cooked crabmeat or 3 cans crabmeat (6 oz each)
  drained, flaked and cartilage removed.

In a large bowl, whisk together first 8 ingredients. Fold in crab. Place the bread crumbs in a shallow dish. Drop 1/3 cup crabmeat mixture; shape into 3/4 inch thick patty. Carefully turn to coat. Repeat with remaining crab mixture. In a skillet, cook patties in butter for 3 minutes or until golden brown.

Meat Loaf
Mrs. Menno Lambright, grandson of M.T. Kuhns

3 lb hamburger	2 c cracker crumbs
1 c milk	1 onion, finely chopped
1 bottle catsup	2 eggs
Salt and pepper to taste	

Mix together and bake at 350 degrees.
When almost done, put one half of the catsup on top.

Mexican Chicken Skillet
Bertha Hershberger

8 chicken drumsticks	2 Tbsp oil
12 oz jar chunky salsa	1/2 c monterey jack cheese
1/2 c broken tortilla chips	

Cook chicken in oil over medium heat 10 to 15 minutes, until brown. Drain. Pour salsa over chicken simmer, covered until tender. Top with cheese, serve with chips.

Mediterranean Macaronada
Theme Buffet: Zorba - Chef Brenda Ritter

1 lb spaghetti
1 c chopped onions
1/2 c shallots
2 tsp salt
1 lb plum tomatoes, quartered
Fresh chopped parsley

1 c olive oil
2 Tbsp minced garlic
1 tsp pepper
Fresh basil
1 Tbsp fennel seed
Grated Romano cheese

Cook spaghetti according to directions. Keep warm.
In saucepan heat oil, onions, garlic, shallots. Cook until translucent. Add pepper, salt, tomatoes and rest of spices. Put spaghetti on serving platter, pour tomato sauce over spaghetti and sprinkle with cheese. Serve immediately.

Mexican Chicken Roll-Ups
Paul Kuhns, great-grandson of M.T. Kuhns

2 1/2 c cooked, debunked chicken
3 tsp taco seasoning
1 can cream of mushroom soup
10 flour tortillas

12 oz sour cream
1 1/2 c shredded cheese
1/2 c salsa

In a bowl, combine chicken, 1/2 cup sour cream, 1 1/2 tsp taco seasoning, half of soup, 1 cup cheese, & salsa. Place 1/3 cup filling on each tortilla. Roll up & place seam side down on greased 13x9 inch baking dish. Combine remaining sour cream, taco seasoning, & soup. Pour over tortillas. Cover & bake at 350 degrees for 30 minutes. Sprinkle with remaining cheese. Serve with additional salsa, chopped lettuce, & chopped tomatoes.

Mexican Lasagna
Cheryl Stichter, great-grandson of M.T. Kuhns

1 lb ground beef (browned)
1/2 can refried beans (optional)
2 large flour tortillas
Tator tots

1 pkg taco seasoning
1 - 8 oz tomato sauce
2 c cheddar-jack cheese

Mix ground beef, taco seasoning, beans, & tomato sauce together.
In 8x8 inch pan layer 1 tortilla, 1/2 ground beef mixture & cheese.
Repeat then top with tator tots. (**Optional** - can add black olives,
onion and tomatoes to beef mixture.) Bake at 350 degrees for 20 to
30 minutes.

Mocked Turkey
Ruth Ann Miller

2 cans cream of chicken soup
1 Tbsp Worcestershire sauce
1 c onion
1/2 box bread stuffing
4 c milk

1 can cream of celery soup
2 lb hamburger, browned
1 loaf bread
Pinch garlic salt

Mix all ingredients and bake at 350 degrees for 1 hour
or until brown

Oatmeal Pancakes
David Mishler, great-great-grandchild of M.T. Kuhns

1 1/2 c quick oats
1 tsp salt
1 tsp soda
3/4 c whole wheat flour

2 c buttermilk
2 eggs, beaten
1 Tbsp maple syrup

Soak oatmeal in buttermilk a short time, add beaten eggs, add rest
of ingredients.

93

Mystery Meatballs
Shirley Pitney

1 1/2 c bread crumbs
3 eggs, beaten
3 lbs ground beef

1/2 c milk
1 pkg dry onion soup

Soak bread crumbs in milk. Add beaten eggs & dry soup mix. Add ground beef & mix well. Add small amounts of salt & pepper. Shape into small balls & place in casserole dish, which has been sprayed with Pam.

Sauce:
12 oz chili sauce
1/2 c brown sugar
16 oz can whole cranberry sauce

1 1/2 c water
16 oz can Sauerkraut, drained

Combine ingredients in saucepan & simmer 5 minutes. Pour sauce over meat mixture. Bake in casserole dish 1 hour at 350 degrees.

Noodles Romanoff
Theme Buffet: Smoke on the Mountain - *Chef Brenda Ritter*

3 lb noodles
3 oz salt
6 oz chopped onion
1/4 tsp garlic powder
4 oz parmesan cheese
2 1/2 c sour cream

3 gallons water
1 Tbsp vegetable oil
1 oz salt
1/4 qt milk
2 lb 8 oz cottage cheese
1 Tbsp paprika

Preheat oven to 350 degrees. On the stove, bring 3 gallons of water and salt to a boil, and cook noodles according to the directions. Drain. In a separate pan, sauté onions with butter until tender. Add flour and seasonings to onions, stirring constantly. Cook 5 to 10 minutes. Add milk gradually to flour mixture, stirring constantly, cook until thickened. Add cottage and parmesan cheeses, sour cream, and paprika. Combine noodles and sauce. Scale pasta mixture into two 12x10x2 inch counter pans. 8 pounds per pan. Sprinkle with cheese. 4 ounces per pan. Bake at 350 degrees for 45 minutes or until heated through.

Pasta
Theme Buffet: Triumph of Love - *Chef Brenda Ritter*

1 lb cooked pasta, your choice

Sauce:

1 c olive oil	1 small onion, diced
1 tsp garlic	1 Tbsp fresh parsley
1 Tbsp fennel seed	1/2 c butter

Combine butter and olive oil. Sauté onion and garlic until translucent, add rest of ingredients, simmer 5 minutes. Pour over pasta.

Pasta With Steamed Mussels
Theme Buffet: Triumph of Love - *Chef Brenda Ritter*

1 1/2 c dry vermouth	1 tsp chopped shallots
1/2 tsp chopped garlic	1/4 tsp white pepper
Juice of 1/2 lemon	1 tsp tarragon
1 Tbsp mint	1/2 tsp parsley
1 tsp oregano	1/2 tsp thyme
5 lbs mussels, washed and debeared	1/2 tsp fennel

In large stainless steel pot combine all ingredients except mussels, bring to a boil. Add mussels when mussels open. Remove pot from heat. Serve immediately.

Pizza Log
Ruth Ann Miller

1 1/2 lb hamburger	3/4 c oatmeal
1 egg	1/4 c onion, chopped
1 tsp salt	1/5 tsp pepper
1 c pizza sauce	16 oz mozzarella cheese

Combine all ingredients. Place in one square cake pan.
Bake at 350 degrees for 1 hour.

Pizza Casserole
Ruth Ann Miller

3 lbs hamburger
1/2 to 3/4 lb spaghetti
2/3 tsp salt
2 tsp baking powder
3 1/2 Tbsp salad dressing
3 c pizza sauce

1 onion, chopped
1 1/3 c flour
1/2 c milk
1/4 c salad oil
2 c grated cheese
1 c sour cream

Fry hamburger w/onion. Cook spaghetti. Mix together flour, baking powder and salt. Add milk and oil all at once and mix well. Press bottom in bottom at 9x13 inch pan. Place hamburger on top of crust then spaghetti and pizza sauce by layers. Mix sour cream, salad dressing and grated cheese together and spread on top. Bake in oven until crust is brown.

Popover Pizza
Ruth Ann Miller

1 lb hamburger, fried
Cheese (enough for topping)
1 Tbsp vegetable oil
2 eggs

1 pt pizza sauce
1 c milk
1 c bisquick

Mix together milk, vegetable oil, bisquick and eggs. In a cake pan place hamburger, sauce, and any other topping (pepperoni, mushrooms, etc) and put bisquick mix on top. Bake in oven until crust is brown.

Poppy Seed Chicken
Rhoda Hershberger

2 lb chicken breasts
1 c sour cream
1 1/2 c crushed Ritz crackers

1 can cream of chicken soup
1 stick butter, melted
Poppy seed

Put chicken breast in buttered 8x8 inch pan. Mix soup and sour cream, pour over chicken. Sprinkle crackers on top, drizzle with butter and sprinkle generously with poppy seed. Bake at 350 degrees for 40 minutes. Double recipe for 13x9 inch pan.

Pork Loin Oatmeal Stout
Theme Buffet: 1776 - Chef Brenda Ritter

3 lb tenderloin	Salt and pepper
Marjoram	1 bottle oatmeal stout

Rub tenderloin with salt, pepper and marjoram. Brown under broiler for 10 minutes. Pull out of oven and reset to bake at 350 degrees. Pour one bottle oatmeal stout over tenderloin. Cover and bake 1 to 1 1/2 hours.

Pork Roast
Theme Buffet: Man of La Mancha - Chef Brenda Ritter

1 whole pork tenderloin	1 Tbsp poultry seasoning
1 Tbsp marjoram	1 Tbsp salt
1/2 Tbsp pepper	

Chutney:

1 small diced onion	1 sliced lime
1 sliced lemon	1 sliced orange
2 c applesauce	1 Tbsp cinnamon
1 tsp cloves	1 tsp nutmeg
1 - 6 oz can orange juice concentrate	

Mix together, add 1 qt apple cider. Cook for 2 hours on simmer. Puree' mixture. Rub tenderloin with herbs and spices. Cook 2 hours at 350 degrees. Baste every 1/2 hour with chutney.

Potato Egg Casserole
Harry Mishler Jr., great-grandson of M.T. Kuhns

4 strips bacon, fried	4 c diced cooked potatoes
3 hard boiled eggs, chopped	1 can cream of chicken soup
1 c milk	Salt & pepper to taste
Minced onion	1/2 c shredded cheese

Crumble fried bacon. Layer potatoes, bacon and eggs in casserole dish. Blend soup, milk, onion, salt and pepper together and pour over top. Sprinkle with cheese. Bake at 350 degrees for 30 minutes. Can substitute diced ham for bacon.

Potato Haystack
Wanda Hershberger, great-granddaughter of M.T.Kuhns

10 to 14 potatoes, boiled, peeled & shredded
2 pkgs Hidden Valley Ranch Mix   2 c sour cream
2 c milk

1 to 2 packages taco seasoning   Salt & pepper
Nacho chips   Cheese sauce

Mix together first 4 ingredients & put in bottom of roaster.
Fry hamburger with some onions & add taco seasoning. Also add
salt & pepper to taste. Put hamburger on top of potato mixture.
Make a cheese sauce & put on top. Bake at 350 degrees for 1 hour.
Before serving crush nacho chips & put on top. (Pepperoni is good
on top of cheese sauce. I use Trio cheese sauce mix to make cheese
sauce.)

Range Beef Stew
Theme Buffet: **Man of La Mancha** - *Chef Brenda Ritter*

2 lb cubed beef   2 onions, quartered
4 carrots, chunked   4 potatoes, chunked
1/2 green pepper

Cover beef with warm water and 2 t beef base. Cover and put in
350 degrees oven for 3 hours. Put beef and vegetables into pot. Add
1 clove garlic and 1 lb fresh mushrooms. Cook for 30 minutes.

Salisbury Steak
Bertha Hershberger

1 can cream of mushroom soup   2 lb ground beef
2/3 c bread crumbs   1 chopped onion
2 eggs, beaten   3/4 c milk
1/4 tsp pepper

Mix all ingredients except soup. Shape meat into patties. Fry in skil
let with a little bit of shortening. Put fried patties in baking dish
and cover with soup. Bake at 350 degrees for 1 hour or until done.

Roast Beef & Yorkshire Pudding
Theme Buffet: My Fair Lady - *Chef Brenda Ritter*

4 lb rib roast   2 Tbsp Oil

Season roast with salt, pepper & garlic the night before cooking. Cover & refrigerate overnight. Preheat oven to 450 degrees. Place beef fat side up. Baste with oil, cook for 1 1/4 hours for rare, 1 1/2 hours for medium. Baste with oil frequently.

Pudding:
3/4 c flour   1/2 tsp salt
3/4 c milk   1 Tbsp water
2 eggs

Sift flour and salt together into mixing bowl. Make a well in the center, add milk and water gradually and beat with wooden spoon. In small bowl beat eggs until fluffy and add to flour mixture and beat until bubbles rise to surface. Pour into a pitcher and put in fridge for 1/2 hour. Remove cooked meat from pan and place on warm platter. Rebeat batter, pour into the hot cooking pan and bake at 450 degrees for 10 minutes. Reduce heat to 350 degrees for 15 minutes or until golden brown. Serve immediately from pan in which it was cooked.

Sarah Ann Casserole
Clara M Helmuth, great-granddaughter of M.T. Kuhns

3 lb hamburger   2 qt green beans
Cheese slices   3 qt mashed potatoes
2 cans cream of mushroom soup   4 oz cream cheese
8 oz sour cream   Milk & salt to suit your taste
4 to 5 c crushed corn flakes   1 stick butter

Fry hamburger & season with taco seasoning, salt & pepper. Put in layers in large roaster, hamburger in bottom, green beans, cover with cheese slices, spread soup over cheese. Spoon mashed potatoes on last, cover with corn flakes & butter. Bake until well heated.

Sausage & Broccoli Quiche
Mrs. Lavern Kuhns, great-grandson of M.T. Kuhns

1 head broccoli, cut up
1 1/2 c sausage, browned
3/4 tsp salt
1 1/3 c milk
3 eggs

2 c cheddar cheese
1/2 c chopped onion
1/4 tsp pepper
3/4 c Bisquick

Cook broccoli for 5 minutes, drain. Mix broccoli, sausage, onion and 1 cup of cheese. Put in a baking pan. Mix rest of ingredients together and pour over broccoli. Bake at 350 degrees for 25 to 30 minutes. Put rest of cheese on top and melt.

Salsa Chicken
Kathy Hockert

1 1/2 c salsa
1 Tbsp mustard

3 Tbsp brown sugar
4 chicken breasts

Mix together salsa, brown sugar and mustard.
Pour over chicken breasts. Bake at 400 degrees for 45 minutes.

Sharp Shooter's Cornish Hen
Theme Buffet: Annie Get Your Gun - *Chef Brenda Ritter*

2 cornish game hens, halved
3 Tbsp olive oil
Salt and pepper to taste
2 Tbsp chopped fresh rosemary

1 c chopped parsley
5 cloves garlic, chopped
1 c white wine

In a small bowl combine the garlic, parsley and 2 Tbsp olive oil. Rinse hens and pat dry. Rub remaining 1 Tbsp olive oil on the inside and outside of the hens. Stuff the garlic and parsley mixture under skin and around each bird. Season with salt and pepper. Place seasoned hens in an airtight, plastic container. Sprinkle with rosemary and pour wine over birds. Cover and refrigerate at least overnight to marinate. Preheat grill for low heat. Remove hens from marinade and place on heated grill. Cook for 45 to 55 minutes or until done.

Sausage Cups
Shirley Pitney

Cups:

1 lb uncooked bulk sausage
2/3 c rolled oats (or saltine crackers)
1/4 c milk

1 Tbsp finely chopped onion
1 egg white

Filling:

8 eggs
1/2 c soft cream cheese (plain or herbed)
3/4 chopped and seeded tomatoes, drained
2 Tbsp snipped fresh chives, dill or green onion tops
Salt and pepper to taste

Preheat oven to 350 degrees. In medium bowl, combine the "cups" ingredients listed above. Divide the mixture evenly into 12 muffin tins. Press mixture firmly around the bottom and sides to form hollow cups. Bake 12 to 15 minutes or until done. Remove from oven, drain cups on paper towels and keep warm. In large skillet, begin scrambling eggs. When almost done, fold in remaining ingredients and finish cooking. Divide the mixture into the sausage cups and serve hot. Makes 12 sausage cups. Refrigerate leftovers.
Note: Sausage cups can be prepared in advance and refrigerated or frozen. Reheat when ready to fill.

Shephard's Pie
Theme Buffet: Brigadoon - Chef Brenda Ritter

1 1/2 lbs ground lamb or beef
1 1/2 c mashed potatoes
1 c brown stock or prepared onion gravy
Salt & pepper to taste

1 med yellow onion, sliced thin
1/2 c diced cooked carrots
2 Tbsp melted butter

Brown onions thoroughly in large skillet or stock pot. Add ground lamb or beef, cook until browned, stirring frequently. Add stock or gravy, make fairly moist to allow absorption when baking. Season to taste. Layer carrots and meat in bottom of deep 5 qt. Casserole dish, spread with mashed potatoes. Drizzle melted butter on top and criss cross with a fork. Bake at 350 degrees for 40 to 45 minutes. Potatoes should form browned, crispy crust.

Sausage Rice Casserole
Judy Beehler

2 lb bulk sausage
3/4 c uncooked long grained rice
2 envelopes Mrs. Grasses soup mix
1 - 4 oz can undrained mushrooms
1 1/2 c diced celery
1 c chopped onion
1/4 tsp salt

Brown sausage in skillet. Remove meat, sauté celery and onion.
Add sausage and rice. Blend in soup mixes with boiling water
(as directed on box), mushrooms and salt. Stir to blend.
Spoon in 3 qt casserole dish. Bake at 350 degrees for 1 1/2 hours.

Scotch Eggs
Brenda Ritter

4 hard boiled eggs
1 egg beaten
2 oz fine white bread crumbs
1 tsp parsley
1/2 lb of sausage meat
Vegetable oil for deep frying
2 level Tbsp plain flour

Dry hard boiled eggs, roll in a little flour, coat with sausage meat.
Roll in flour, coat with egg, roll in bread crumbs. Fry in a deep fat
frying pan for 10 minutes until golden. Pat with kitchen towel to
remove excess fat. Cut in two and garnish with parsley.

Scrambled Egg Muffins
Mrs. Glen Hostetler, great-grandson of M.T. Kuhns

1/2 lb sausage
1/2 c chopped onions
1/2 tsp salt
1/4 tsp garlic powder
12 eggs
1/4 c green peppers
1/4 tsp pepper
1/2 c cheddar cheese

Brown sausage. In a bowl beat eggs. Add onions, green peppers,
salt, black pepper, & garlic powder. Stir in sausage & cheese.
Spoon by 1/3 cupfuls in a greased muffin cup. Bake at 350 degrees
for 20 to 25 minutes. Makes 1 dozen.

Short Ribs
Theme Buffet: **Annie Get Your Gun** - *Chef Brenda Ritter*

1 Tbsp ground cumin	1 Tbsp chili powder
1 Tbsp paprika	Salt and pepper to taste
3 lbs baby back ribs	1 c Bulls Eye barbeque sauce

Preheat gas grill for high heat. In a small jar, combine cumin, chili powder, paprika and salt & pepper. Place lid on jar and mix well. Trim off the membrane sheath from the back of each rack. Sprinkle as much of rub onto both sides of the ribs as desired. Place tin foil on lower rack to capture drippings and prevent flare-ups. Brush grate with oil and lay ribs on top rack of grill. Reduce heat to low, shut grill and leave undisturbed for 1 hour. Do not lift lid. Brush ribs with barbecue sauce and grill additional 5 minutes.

Shrimp and Garlic Pasta
Theme Buffet: **Hello, Dolly!** - *Chef Brenda Ritter*

1 Tbsp olive oil	1 tsp Rose's garlic, chopped
3 Tbsp scallions, chopped	50 to 70 - 4 oz shrimp
5 oz pasta fettuccine, cooked	Pinch seasoning salt
Pinch of red pepper flakes	1 oz fresh mushrooms, sliced
2 oz asparagus spears, cut in thirds	1 oz lobster base
1 qt hot water	

Heat hot water to boil and add base. Bring to a boil and remove. Set aside. Sauté shrimp and pepper flakes in oil for 1 minute. Add mushrooms, asparagus, scallions, seasoning salt and garlic. Cook 1 minute. Add pasta and toss well. Add 2 oz of lobster stock to pasta and heat through. Serve in arcorc pasta bowl with under liner. Garnish with parmesan cheese and parsley.

Southern Fried Catfish
Theme Buffet: **Fiddler on the Roof** - *Chef Brenda Ritter*

6 catfish fillets	2 c Drakes fry mix
1 tsp pepper	2 Tbsp Old Bay seasonings

Bread catfish in mixture. Fry until golden brown.

Silicone Meatloaf
Greg and Marsolie Kuhns, great-grandson of M.T. Kuhns

2 beaten eggs
1/2 c tomato juice
1/4 tsp salt
1 tsp minced garlic
1 1/2 c shredded mozzarella cheese

1 slice soft bread crumbs
1/2 tsp dried oregano
1/4 tsp pepper
2 lbs lean ground beef
8 thin slices of boiled ham

Mix together all ingredients, except ham & cheese. (I divide into 2 amounts) Pat each into a rectangle on waxed paper. Lay ham onto meat mixture. Cover with cheese. Using the waxed paper, start at long edge & roll jelly roll fashion. Seal end, seam side down. Bake a 350 degrees for 1 1/4 hours. Center will be pink due to the ham.

Sloppy Joes
Susan Nunemaker

2 Tbsp butter
1/2 c celery, minced
1 1/2 lb hamburger
1 c chili sauce
1/2 c water

1/2 onions, minced
1 c chopped green peppers
1 c mushrooms
1/4 c ketchup

Heat butter in skillet, add onions, celery, peppers and suite. When these are limp, add, extra lean ground beef & cook, stir until meat i lightly browned, then add rest of ingredients. Season to taste. Simmer uncovered on low heat about 15 minutes. Serves 8.

Tavern Crab Cakes
Theme Buffet: 1776 - Chef Brenda Ritter

1 egg, beaten
2 Tbsp tomato catsup
1/2 tsp salt
2 hard boiled eggs, chopped

1 c flaked cooked crab meat
1 green pepper, chopped
1 tsp chili powder

Blend together. Shape into patties. Cook in butter until golden brown.

Smoked Haddock Fish Cakes
Theme Buffet: My Fair Lady - *Chef Brenda Ritter*

4 Tbsp stale bread crumbs
2 c cooked mashed potatoes
2 hard boiled eggs, chopped
1/4 tsp tarragon vinegar
Salt & pepper to taste

1 lb cooked haddock, flaked
1 raw egg
1/4 tsp lemon juice
1 Tbsp chopped parsley
1/2 tsp turmeric flour

Combine in mixing bowl fish, mashed potatoes and raw egg. When well mixed add hard boiled eggs, lemon juice, vinegar, parsley and turmeric. Season with salt and pepper. Mixture will be sticky and should be shaped into little round cakes. To do this dip fingers in flour, roll each cake in breadcrumbs, cover and refrigerate at least 2 hours. Fry in small amount of oil over medium heat until golden brown.

Stir Fried Vegetables and Chicken
Menno and Esther Kuhns, grandson of M.T. Kuhns

1/2 large chicken breast
1 c thinly sliced carrots
1 1/2 c cooked rice or noodles
Other sliced vegetables of choice may be added

1 c sliced onion
1 1/2 c broccoli florets
2 c shredded cabbage

Cut chicken breast into bite size pieces and soak in soy sauce enough to bathe each piece. Sauté each ingredient separately in skillet with oil, should be crispy when done. Pour each ingredient into saucepan or casserole dish. When all are done add soy sauce, salt and pepper to taste. Stir lightly until mixed together. Serve over rice or noodles.

Souper Meat-n-Potato Pie
Kristine Hochstetler, great-granddaughter of M.T. Kuhns

1 lb ground beef
1 egg
2 Tbsp chopped parsley
Dash of pepper
1 can cream mushroom soup

1/4 c onion, chopped
1/4 c fine bread crumbs
1/4 tsp salt
2 c mashed potatoes
1/4 c shredded mild cheese

Mix thoroughly 1/2 can of the soup, beef, onion, egg, parsley, & seasonings. Press firmly into 9 inch pie plate. Bake at 350 degrees for 25 minutes. Spoon off fat. Frost with mashed potatoes, top with other 1/2 can soup & cheese. Bake 10 more minutes, or until hot.

Stromboli
Rhoda Hershberger

1 loaf frozen bread dough, thaw
1/4 lb sliced cooked salami
1 1/4 lb white American cheese
1 c sliced cooked green peppers
1 c sliced onion
Oregano and sweet basil

1/4 lb thin sliced hard salami
1/4 lb thin sliced ham
1/4 lb mozzarella cheese
1 c cooked mushrooms
1 c grated parmesan cheese

Divide bread dough in half. Grease two large cookie sheets. Roll out dough to cover pans. Half of dough to each pan. Sprinkle with herbs. Arrange meats, cheese, and vegetables in alternate layers up center of dough. Sprinkle last layer with parmesan cheese and moderate amounts of herbs. Fold dough up over center and pinch ends to seal. Bake at 350 degrees for approximately 30 minutes.

Turkey
Amish Acres Thresher Dinner

1 - 15 lb turkey
1/2 c salt
1 Tbsp thyme

1/2 c seasoned salt
1 1/2 Tbsp ground mustard
1 1/2 Tbsp garlic salt

Baste thawed turkey with butter or oil and sprinkle with turkey salt. Cook in 350 degree oven until golden brown.

Stuffed Ham Sandwiches
Brenda Beehler

1 loaf unsliced Italian bread
1/3 c parsley, chopped
1/2 c shredded cheddar cheese
2 Tbsp finely chopped onion

1/3 c Miracle Whip
8 oz cream cheese
Thinly sliced ham
1 large dill pickle

Split bread lengthwise, hollow out each half with a fork, leaving 1/3 inch thick shell. Spread Miracle Whip over hollow of loaf and sprinkle with parsley. Blend cheeses, celery, onion and salt in a bowl and spoon in halves of bread, packing down well, leaving hollow center. Quarter pickle lengthwise and roll each quarter in thinly sliced ham. Place rolls end to end in bread and place remainder of ham in cavity. Put top on and wrap tightly. Chill and serve by cutting into slices about 1/2 inch thick. Make a day ahead for better blending.

Turkey Enchiladas
Pauline Kaufman, great-granddaughter of M.T. Kuhns

1 can (4 oz) green chilies, drained & chopped
3 Tbsp butter divided
1/3 c taco seasoning
2 Tbsp flour
1/2 c tomatoes fresh, chopped
2 1/2 cooked, cubed turkey
2 c shredded cheddar cheese divided

1/2 c chopped onions
1 c sour cream (divided)
1/8 tsp chili powder
10 flour tortillas
1 c chicken or turkey broth

In glass bowl combine the onions, 2 Tbsp Chilies, 1 Tbsp Butter. Cook for a few minutes. Add taco sauce, 1/4 cup sour cream & chili powder. Stir in turkey & 1/2 c. cheese. Divide the mixture among tortillas. Roll tortillas place seam side down in 13x9 inch baking dish. Melt 2 Tbsp butter, blend in flour, then slowly stir in broth. Cook until thickened. Stirring constantly. Stir in remaining sour cream & chilies. Pour over enchiladas. Bake 45 minutes at 325 degrees. Put cheese on and heat until melted.

Taco Grande
Brenda Beehler

1 pound ground beef (or turkey)	1 package taco seasoning
1 jar (16 oz.) salsa	8 flour tortilla shells
2 c shredded co-jack cheese	1 green onion, chopped
4 c shredded lettuce	1/2 c sour cream

Spray bottom of deep dish baking pan. In frying pan, brown hamburger & drain grease. Add taco mix & water and cook as directed on pkg. Remove from heat & stir in 1 cup of salsa. Arrange 4 tortillas on bottom of baking dish. Spoon meat mixture over tortillas, top with 1 cup cheese and onion. Place remaining tortillas on top & spread remaining salsa over shells, sprinkle with remaining cheese and onion. Bake 30 minutes at 350 degrees. Cut into wedges and garnish with lettuce and sour cream.

Tandoori Chicken
Theme Buffet: **Brigadoon** - *Chef Brenda Ritter*

12 chicken drumsticks or bread pieces, skinless

1 c plain yogurt	1 1/2 Tbls red chili powder
2 Tbsp coriander powder	1 Tbsp garlic powder
1 Tbsp ginger powder	1 Tbsp cumin powder
1/2 Tbsp garam masala	2 Tbsp salt

Tandoori in Indian stands for an earthen oven which is sort of cylindrical and uses coal as the fuel. This recipe will need a BBQ grill as a substitute. Gas or electric oven may be used, but it will lose most of its flavor. Chicken has to be marinated for at least 6 hours, ideally overnight. Prick the chicken pieces with a fork all over, apply the tenderizer to the chicken pieces and let stand for an hour or so.

Marinade: Take a wide and deep bowl, large enough to hold all the chicken pieces. Add the yogurt plus one cup water and all the spices. Mix well so all spices are blended together. Add the chicken pieces, mix until all pieces are covered. Cover the bowl with a lid and let stand 6 hours. Put in refrigerator if you want to marinate it longer. When ready to grill, apply melted butter to the chicken pieces with a brush. Place on grill in normal fashion, turn over chicken pieces when they look brownish red in color.

Weiner Schnitzel with Spaetzle
Theme Buffet: **The Sound of Music** - *Chef Brenda Ritter*

1 1/2 lb veal scallops
2 eggs, beaten
1 lemon, thinly sliced

1/4 tsp salt
1 c butter

Pound scallops gently to an even 1/8 inch thickness. Combine flour, salt and pepper; dip scallops in flour, then eggs and bread crumbs. Melt butter in large skillet until very hot; fry scallops, a few at a time, until golden brown. Remove scallops to a heated platter. Add lemon juice to pan drippings, cool 2 to 3 minutes. Pour over scallops and garnish with lemon slices.

Spaetzle

2 eggs, beaten
1/8 tsp nutmeg
1/8 tsp pepper
1/4 c lemon juice
1/4 tsp salt

1 1/2 c all purpose flour
1 c all purpose flour
1 c dried bread crumbs
1/2 c milk
2 Tbsp butter

Combine eggs and milk, stir in flour, salt and nutmeg, beating until smooth. Drop dough by teaspoons into nutmeg, beating until smooth. Drop dough by teaspoons into boiling water, boil for 2 to 3 minutes. Drain and toss with butter or melt butter in skillet and gently fry spaetzle until brown, about 3 to 4 minutes.

Weiner-Bean Bake
Fannie Mae Stichter, granddaughter of M.T. Kuhns

1 - 10 oz pkg frozen lima beans
1 - 1 lb can kidney beans
1/4 c molasses
1/2 envelope Worcestershire sauce
1/2 envelope dry onion soup mix
1 lb frankfurters, cut in 1" pieces

1 - 1 lb can pork & beans
1/2 c chili sauce
1/2 to 1 tsp dry mustard

Cook limas according to package directions; drain. Mix with pork & beans & kidney beans. Stir in remaining ingredients. Put into 2 quart casserole or bean pot. Bake covered in 350 degrees oven for 1 hour. Uncover; stir & continue baking 30 minutes. Makes 6 servings.

Wet Burritos

Lamar and Ruby Miller, great-grandson of M.T. Kuhns

1 1/2 lb hamburger
1 can cream of mushroom soup
1 can refried beans
1 package taco seasoning

1 onion, chopped
1 - 16 oz sour cream
1 package soft tortilla shells
4 c shredded cheese

Brown meat and onions, drain. Follow directions on taco seasoning package and add to hamburger. Add beans. Mix sour cream and soup together, spread 1/2 of mixture in bottom of cake pan. Fill shells with meat and roll up and put in pan. Spread remaining soup mixture on top of shells. Top with cheese. Bake at 350 degrees for 15 to 20 minutes or until cheese is melted. Serve with lettuce and tomatoes.

Wigglers Casserole

Mrs. Norman Kuhns, great-grandson of M.T. Kuhns

3 lb hamburger
3 c celery, diced
3 c spaghetti
9 slices bacon
2 cans cream of mushroom soup
1 qt tomato juice

3 onions, chopped
3 c carrots, diced
1 lb Velveeta cheese
3 c potatoes, raw & diced
3 cans peas

Heat hamburger & onion in pan. Pour into roaster & add cooked vegetables and spaghetti. Fry bacon & add to mushroom soup, tomato juice and cheese. Mix all together. Bake at 350 degrees for 1 1/2 hours. Serves 10 to 12.

Zucchini Bake
Gloria Fimbianti

3 c chopped, peeled zucchini
1 c Bisquick
1/2 c grated parmesan cheese
1/2 tsp parsley
Salt & pepper to taste

1 onion, chopped fine
1/2 c oil
1/2 tsp oregano
4 eggs, beaten

Mix all ingredients together, adding eggs last. Pour into 9x9 inch buttered pan. Bake at 350 degrees for 30 minutes. Double recipe for 9x13 inch pan.

Zucchini Squash Casserole
Mrs. Jonas Kuhns

3 c zucchini squash, raw & grated
4 eggs
1/2 c grated cheese
Salt & pepper

1/2 c vegetable oil
1/2 c chopped onion
4 hot dogs
Parsley (optional)

Beat eggs with vegetable oil. Mix in all the other ingredients. Bake uncovered at 350 degrees for 1 hour.

111

Desserts
Pies

Andrea's Fruit Pizza
Andrea Stahly

Crust:
1 tube Pillsbury cookie dough

Frosting:
1 - 8 oz cream cheese (regular or low fat) 1 c powdered sugar
1 tsp vanilla

Fruit topping:
Your choice, Apples, bananas, cherries, pineapple, strawberries, blueberries, mangos, oranges, grapes, starfruit, peaches, apricots, pears, etc.

Bake cookie according to package directions in a 9x13 inch baking pan. Mix together the cream cheese, powdered sugar and vanilla in a medium bowl and set aside. Dice all fruit and set aside. Once the crust has cooled COMPLETELY, spread cream cheese mix evenly over cookie crust. Spread fruit out evenly over cream cheese. Best if served right out of fridge and with a tall glass of milk.

Apple Pandowdy
Amish Acres Kitchen

4 tart apples (like Granny Smith)   1/2 cup molasses
2 Tbsp butter   Biscuit dough (Jiffy or Bisquick)
1/2 tsp cinnamon

Core and slice apples and put them in a greased pie dish. Sprinkle with cinnamon, drizzle on molasses, and dot with butter. Cover with biscuit dough rolled out to about 1/2 inch in thickness. Cut vents so steam can escape. Bake at 375 degrees for 30 minutes. Serve hot cutting squares of biscuit as a base for the fruit mixture. Serve with whipped cream sprinkled with nutmeg.

Instead of rolling out the dough, drop it from a spoon over the filling. This allows the gooey sauce to bubble up around the dough.

Blueberry Cream Pie
Chris Townsend

3 c blueberries
1/2 c sugar
3/4 c milnot
1/3 Tbsp cinnamon

8 inch unbaked pie shell
1/4 tsp salt
3 Tbsp flour

Put blueberries in pie shell. Mix remaining ingredients and pour over blueberries. Bake at 400 degrees for 35 to 45 minutes. Serve with whipped topping.

Bob Andy Pie
Mrs. R. Lehman, great-granddaughter of M.T. Kuhns

1/2 c flour
1/2 tsp cinnamon
2 eggs, separated

1/4 tsp cloves
1 c white sugar
2 c milk

Mix flour, spices, & sugar. Add part of milk and egg yolks. Scald rest of milk & add. Beat egg whites until foamy and add to above. Pour into a 9 inch unbaked pie shell. Bake at 425 degrees for 10 minutes

Bob Andy Pie
Elizabeth M. Schrock, granddaughter of M.T. Kuhns

2 c sugar
1/2 tsp cloves
3 beaten egg yolks
3 beaten egg whites

1 heaping tsp cinnamon
1 Tbsp butter
2 c sweet milk

Mix all together except egg whites. Beat egg whites then fold into rest of ingredients. Makes 2 pies.

Boston Cream Pie
Theme Buffet: 1776 - Chef Brenda Ritter

6 Tbsp butter, softened	2 Tbsp all-purpose flour
1 1/2 c cake flour	2 tsp baking powder
1/4 tsp salt	3/4 c sugar
2 eggs	1 tsp vanilla extract
1/2 c milk	1/2 c light cream
1/2 c milk	1/4 c sugar
1 pinch salt	4 tsp cornstarch
2 eggs	1/2 tsp vanilla extract
3 - 1 oz squares semisweet chocolate	2 Tbsp butter
1/4 c light cream	1/2 tsp vanilla extract
1/2 c confectioners sugar	

Grease and flour two 9 inch round cake pans. Sift the all-purpose flour, cake flour, baking powder and salt together and set aside. In a deep bowl cream 6 Tbsp of butter with 3/4 cup sugar until light and fluffy. Beat in the 2 eggs, one at a time, then beat in the 1 t vanilla extract. Add the flour mixture alternately with the 1/2 c of the milk in 3 additions, beating the batter smooth after each addition. Divide the batter between the 2 prepared pans. Bake at 375 degrees for 15 minutes or until cakes begin to shrink away from the sides of the pan. Turn cakes onto wire racks to cool. **To make filling:** Combine the 1/2 c light cream with 1/4 c milk and cook over medium heat until bubbles begin to form around the edge of the pan. Immediately add 1/4 c of the sugar and salt, stirring until dissolved. Remove pan from heat. In a small bowl combine 1/4 c milk with the cornstarch and whisk to remove lumps. Whisk in the 2 eggs. Add hot cream mixture in a thin stream, whisking constantly. Return mixture to the saucepan, bring to a boil and cook over low heat, stirring constantly until the custard thickens and is smooth. Remove from heat and stir in the 1/2 t vanilla and allow to cool to room temp. **To make chocolate frosting:** In a heavy saucepan over low heat, stir the chocolate pieces and 2 Tbsp butter until they are completely melted. Remove from heat and stir constantly, add the 1/4 c light cream in a thin steady stream. When mixture is smooth, stir in the confectioners sugar and beat vigorously. Stir in the 1/2 t vanilla. **To assemble cake:** Spread the cooled filling over one of the cooled cakes and place the second cake on top. Pour the chocolate frosting evenly over the top allowing it to spill down the sides.

Buttermilk Coconut Pie
Mrs. David A. Schrock

1 1/4 c sugar	2 Tbsp flour
1/2 c butter, melted	3 eggs, beaten
1/2 c buttermilk	1 tsp vanilla
3 1/2 oz coconut	1 unbaked pie shell

Combine the sugar & flour in a large bowl. Add melted butter, eggs, buttermilk, vanilla and 2/3 of the coconut. Mix well. Pour mixture into pie shell. Sprinkle with remaining coconut. Bake at 325 degrees for 65 minutes or until set. Option: Sprinkle a little nutmeg on top.

Carmel Custard Pie
Ruth Ann Miller

1 1/2 c brown sugar	1 egg, beaten
2 tsp flour, heaping	2 c milk

In a bowl combine brown sugar and egg. Add flour and milk. Bake at 400 degrees (sometimes lower if bubbles are on top of pie). Cook till set.

Chocolate Malt Shoppe Pie
Kathy Stricter, great-granddaughter of M.T. Kuhns

1 1/2 c chocolate cookie crumbs	1/4 c butter
1 pint vanilla ice cream, softened	2 Tbsp milk, divided
1/2 c crushed malted milk balls	1 c whipping cream
3 Tbsp instant chocolate malted milk powder	
3 Tbsp marshmallow crème	

Combine crumbs & butter. Press into a 9 inch pie pan. Freeze while preparing filling. In a bowl, blend ice cream, crushed malted milk balls and 1 Tbsp milk. Spoon into crust. Freeze for 1 hour. Meanwhile blend malted milk powder, marshmallow crème and remaining milk. Stir in whipped cream. Whip until soft peaks form. Spread over ice cream layer. Freeze several hours. Garnish with additional whipped cream and malted milk balls.

Chocolate Peanut Butter Pie
Linda Schrock, great-granddaughter of M.T. Kuhns

1 - 8 oz cream cheese	1/2 c peanut butter
1 c powdered sugar	2 c whipped toppings
1 qt water	1 pt cream
1 c sugar	2 Tbsp cocoa
4 Tbsp mira clear	6 small peanut butter cups
2 baked pie crusts	Additional whipped topping

Heat 1 qt water. Stir together sugar, cocoa and mira clear and add cream. Stir into heated water and cook until thick. Boil 1 minute. Cool. Mix first 4 ingredients together and put a thin layer in bottom of pie crust. Finish filling crust with the chocolate filling. Top with whipped topping and garnish with peanut butter cups cut in half and placed in a circle.

Creamy Lemon Pie
Jenni Pletcher-Wysong

1 3/4 c cold milk
2 packages Jello vanilla flavored instant pudding
1 can frozen lemonade concentrate, thawed
1 tub Cool Whip, thawed
Graham cracker crust

Pour milk into large bowl. Add pudding mixes. Beat with whisk 30 seconds. Add lemonade concentrate. Beat with a whisk 30 seconds (mix will be thick). Immediately stir in whipped topping. Spoon into crust and refrigerate 4 hours. You can double everything and it fits into a compote for a layered dessert. Use graham cracker crumbs instead of pie crust.

Dutch Apple Pie
Amish Acres Kitchen

4 to 6 baking Apples   1 cup water
1/2 to 3/4 cup sugar (depending on sweetness)
3 Tbsp Clearjel or cornstarch   1/3 c water
1/2 tsp cinnamon   1 Tbsp margarine

Peel and slice 4 to 6 baking apples. Add 1 cup water and then
1/2 cup - 3/4 cup of sugar, depending on the sweetness of the
apple. Bring to a boil in saucepan. Cook just a couple of minutes
until softened, but not mushy. Dissolve Clearjel or cornstarch in
1/3 cup water, stirring until thickened. Remove from heat and stir
in cinnamon and butter. Pour into unbaked pie crust and top with
crumb topping.

Topping:
3/4 c flour   1/4 c brown sugar
3 Tbsp margarine

Mix flour and brown sugar, cut in margarine.

Fresh Fruit Pie
Edith Kuhns, great-granddaughter of M.T. Kuhns

1 c sugar   1 c water
1 Tbsp lemon juice   1 Tbsp Karo syrup
3 Tbsp Clear-Jel   3 Tbsp Jell-O
2 1/2 c fruit

Cook until clear, add jello until dissolved. Cook. Add fruit.
For Strawberry pie use strawberry Jell-O, for blueberry use lemon
Jell-O, for peach use peach or apricot Jell-O etc.

Fresh Strawberry Pie
Laura Slabaugh

9 inch baked pie shell (cooled)	1 c sugar
3 Tbsp clear jel or cornstarch	Pinch of salt
2 1/2 c fresh whole strawberries	1/2 c water
1 c lightly crushed strawberries with juice red food color	

Combine clear jell, sugar, water and salt. Mix well. Add crushed strawberries and coloring. Cook over medium heat until thick stirring constantly. Remove from heat and cool slightly then pour over berries and chill until firm. Serve with whipped cream or ice cream.

German Sweet Chocolate Pie
Amish Acres Kitchen

4 oz German sweet chocolate	1/4 c butter
1 1/2 c sugar	1/8 tsp salt
13 oz can evaporated milk	1 1/3 c coconut
2 eggs, beaten	1 tsp vanilla
1 unbaked pie crust	1/2 c pecans

Melt chocolate with butter over low heat, stirring until blended. Remove from heat; gradually blend in sugar, milk and salt thoroughly. Beat in eggs and vanilla. Gradually blend in chocolate mixture. Pour into pie shell. Combine coconut and nuts and sprinkle over filling. Bake at 375 degrees for 45 to 50 minutes until puffed and browned. (Filling will be soft, but will set while cooling)

Grapenut Pie
Marlene Hershberger, great-granddaughter of M.T. Kuhns

1/2 c grapenuts	1/2 c warm water
3 eggs	3/4 c sugar
3/4 c Karo corn syrup	1/4 c maple syrup
3 Tbsp butter	1 tsp vanilla
1/8 tsp salt	

Combine cereal & water, let set. Mix everything else together then fold in cereal. Bake at 350 degrees.

Huckleberry Finn Pie
Theme Buffet: Big River - *Chef Brenda Ritter*

1 - 9 inch double pie crust
3/4 c white sugar
1 tsp grated lemon rind
2 Tbsp butter
2 tsp white sugar

4 cups huckleberries
1 Tbsp all-purpose flour
2 Tbsp lemon juice
2 Tbsp whipping cream

Place huckleberries in pastry lined pan. In a small bowl mix together 3/4 cup sugar and flour. Spoon over berries. Sprinkle lemon rind and lemon juice over top. Dot with butter. Cover with top crust. Seal edges and cut steam vents in top. Brush surface with whipping cream, avoiding fluted edges of crust. Sprinkle with 2 t sugar. Bake at 425 degrees for 15 minutes. Reduce heat to 350 degrees and bake additional 20 to 25 minutes until crust is golden brown.

Instant Cheese Pie
Sarah Kuhns, great-granddaughter of M.T. Kuhns

Graham cracker crumb crust 8 oz cream cheese (softened)
1 1/3 c half & half or cream whipped
3 1/4 oz package instant vanilla pudding

Filling: Cherry, raspberry, blueberry, or whatever fruit you wish. Blend cream cheese until smooth. Gradually beat in half & half until creamy. Add pudding mix until smooth. Pour into crust. Chill until set. Put filling on top & serve.

Katy Maud Pletcher's Gone with the Wind Pie
Lenore Pletcher

1 1/2 c sugar
2 eggs
1/2 c milk
1/4 tsp nutmeg

1/2 c butter
1 Tbsp flour
1 tsp cinnamon

Mix sugar and butter, then add remaining ingredients. Put in a 9 inch pie shell. Bake at 350 degrees for 30 to 45 minutes.

Lemon Sponge Pie
Fannie Kuhns, granddaughter of M.T. Kuhns

Juice & rind of 1 lemon
3 Tbsp flour
1/2 tsp salt
1 1/2 c hot water or milk

1 c sugar
3 eggs, separated
2 Tbsp butter
Pastry for 1 crust

Cream butter, add sugar & egg yolks. Beat well, add milk, flour, salt, lemon juice, grated rind & water or milk. Fold in stiffly beaten egg whites. Pour in unbaked pie shell. Bake at 325 degrees for 40 to 45 minutes. Makes 1 pie.

Lemonade Pie
Ruth Ann Miller

1 - 6 oz lemonade, frozen
1 Tbsp lemon juice
Graham cracker crust

1 can Eagle brand milk
8 oz Cool Whip

Mix the lemonade, milk and lemon juice. Blend in cool whip. Put in a graham cracker crust. Let set in refrigerator for 3 hours.

Mississippi Muddy Water Pie
Theme Buffet: Big River - *Chef Brenda Ritter*

Pastry for single crust pie

Filling:
2 oz unsweetened chocolate, coarsely chopped
1 oz semisweet chocolate, coarsely chopped
1 Tbsp instant coffee granules
3 large eggs
1/4 c light corn syrup

1 stick butter
1 c plus 2 Tbsp sugar
1 tsp vanilla

Heat oven to 350 degrees. Make filling in medium saucepan. Melt both chocolates with butter and coffee over low heat. Stir until smooth, remove from heat and cool slightly. In medium bowl whisk together eggs, sugar, corn syrup and vanilla. Whisk in chocolate mixture until well blended. Pour into crust. Bake until filling puffs and top is cracked and slightly crisp. (Approx. 45 minutes)

© Amish Acres, Nappanee, Indiana

Old Fashion Cream Pie
Mrs. Martha Miller, granddaughter of M.T. Kuhns

2 c whipping cream	3 c milk
1 1/2 c brown sugar	1/2 c white sugar
1/4 c margarine	2/3 c flour
1 tsp vanilla	1 pinch of salt

Bring to boiling whipped cream, 1 cup milk and margarine. Meanwhile mix together rest of ingredients except rest of milk. Pour boiling mixture over other ingredients. Mix well, then add rest of milk. Stir and pour into 2 unbaked pie shells. Sprinkle with nutmeg. Bake 400 degrees until set like custard or won't shake when moved. Approximately 30 minutes.

Pecan Pie
Chris Townsend

1 c chopped pecans	20 Ritz crackers, rolled fine
1 c sugar	3 egg whites, beaten stiff
1 Tbsp vanilla	

Mix pecans, 1/2 c sugar and crackers. Fold egg whites, 1/2 c sugar and vanilla. Fold step 1 and step 2 together and place in a buttered pie pan. Bake at 350 degrees for 25 minutes. Cool, spread with cool whip. Refrigerate.

Peppermint Ice Cream Pie
Ruth Ann Miller

2 c crushed Oreo cookies	5 Tbsp melted butter
2 c peppermint ice cream, softened	1 c Cool Whip
1/3 c crushed peppermint candies	

Combine Oreo cookies and butter, press into slightly greased pan. Mix together ice cream, cool whip and peppermint candies. Mix well and pour over crust. Freeze.

Peppermint Stick Pie
Laura Slabaugh

4 1/2 c crisp rice cereal
1 c (16 oz) semisweet chocolate chips, melted
2 qts peppermint stick ice cream, softened
Chocolate syrup or chocolate fudge topping
Crushed peppermint candies

Combine cereal and chocolate chips. Mix well. Press into bottom and up sides of a ungreased 10 inch pie pan. Freeze 5 minutes. Spoon ice cream into crust. Freeze until ready to serve. Garnish with syrup and peppermint candies.

Pumpkin - Gingersnap Pie
Amish Acres Kitchen

4 oz serving size vanilla pudding
2 tsp pumpkin pie spice
3/4 c chopped pecans
1/2 c pumpkin
1 graham cracker crust

3/4 c cream
1/2 c whipped topping
3/4 c milk
1 c crushed gingersnaps

Make vanilla pudding as directed on box, before cooking add pumpkin pie spice. After it's cooked add pumpkin. Cover with plastic wrap. Let stand for a couple of hours or overnight. When ready to put in pie shell fold in topping and coarsely crushed gingersnaps. Sprinkle 1/2 c pecans on bottom of prepared pie crust. Put pumpkin mixture into prepared pie crust. Sprinkle with remaining pecans and garnish with additional gingersnap crumbs. Cover, chill in fridge for a couple of hours.

Pumpkin Pie
Mattie Mishler, granddaughter of M.T. Kuhns

6 eggs, separated
3 tsp pumpkin pie spice
3 heaping Tbsp flour
3/4 c white sugar

1 pint pumpkin
1 1/2 tsp salt
1 1/2 c brown sugar
5 c milk

Beat egg yolks then add all ingredients. Beat egg whites and add to mixture as a last step. Pour into pie crust and bake until firm.

Pumpkin Pie
Regina Mishler, great-great-grandchild of M.T.Kuhns

4 c pumpkin
3 c milk (scalded)
1 1/2 tsp ginger
1 1/2 tsp salt
1 Tbsp clear-jell

6 eggs, beaten
3 tsp cinnamon
3/4 tsp cloves
2 1/4 c sugar

Mix spices with sugar so it will dissolve better. Mix together everything else. Pour into 3 unbaked pie shells. Bake at 400 degrees for 10 minutes, then at 350 degrees for 45 minutes, till they crack open on top.

Pumpkin Pie
Mrs. Roman Harshberger, granddaughter of M.T. Kuhns

1 c cooked pumpkin
2 Tbsp flour
1/2 tsp cinnamon
1 1/2 c milk

1 egg
1/2 tsp allspice
1/2 c sugar

Mix & put in dough lined pie pan. This is for 1 pie.

Shoofly Pie
Amish Acres Thresher Dinner

1 1/4 c flour
1/2 tsp cinnamon
3 Tbsp vegetable oil
3/4 c boiling water
1/4 c light molasses
9 inch unbaked pie shell

1/2 c brown sugar
1/4 tsp salt
1/2 tsp baking soda
1/2 c dark corn syrup
1 large egg, well beaten

Combine flour, sugar, cinnamon and salt. Blend in oil, set aside. Dissolve baking soda in boiling water. Stir in corn syrup and molasses. Let mixture cool. Add egg. Sprinkle 1/2 c flour mixture into unbaked pastry shell. Carefully cover with liquid filling. Top with remaining flour mixture. Bake at 375 degrees for 25 to 30 minutes or until the mixture sets. Makes 1 pie.

Strawberry Pie
Mrs. Ben Kuhns, great grandson of M.T. Kuhns

1 c sugar
1/4 c cornstarch
1/4 tsp salt
4 c sliced strawberries

1 1/2 c water
1 Tbsp lemon juice
3 oz strawberry Jell-O

Cook sugar, cornstarch, & water until thick & clear.
Add lemon juice, salt, & strawberry Jell-O. Cool then add strawberries. Pour filling into baked pie crust. Refrigerate 2 to 3 hours. Top with whipped cream & enjoy.

Sweetheart Pie
Leonna (Kuhns) Stutzman

18 graham crackers   1/2 c melted butter
1/2 c sugar

Custard:
3 eggs, separated   1/2 c sugar
4 tsp cornstarch   2 c milk
1 1/2 tsp vanilla or season with nutmeg

Roll crackers fine. Add sugar & melted butter, blend. Keep 1 cup of this mixture for the top of pie. **Custard for filling as follows:** Beat egg yolks with sugar & cornstarch. Gradually add milk. Cook slowly until thick. Add flavoring. Put this in crumb lined pan. Beat whites stiff & add 1 Tbsp sugar. Spread this on top of custard. Cover with remaining crumbs. Bake at 350 degrees for 30 minutes.

Vermont Maple Cream Pie
Theme Buffet: The Sound of Music - Chef Brenda Ritter

3 pints heavy cream   12 Tbsp sugar
6 Tbsp flour   1/2 tsp salt
6 egg whites, slightly beaten   1 Tbsp maple flavoring

In double boiler heat cream. Mix sugar, flour and salt. Pour hot cream over mixture and bring back to the double boiler. Cook until thickened, remove from heat and add egg whites. Pour into pastry shells. Bake at 400 degrees for 15 minutes.

Desserts
Cakes

3 Step Caramel Pecan Cheesecake
Andrea Stahly

2 - 8 oz packages cream cheese	1/2 c sugar
1/2 tsp vanilla	2 eggs
1 graham cracker crust	20 caramels
2 Tbsp milk	1/2 c chopped nuts

Mix cream cheese, sugar and vanilla with mixer. Add eggs, mix well. Melt caramels with milk. Stir in pecans. Pour over caramels into crust. Top with cream cheese batter. Bake at 350 degrees. Cool. Refrigerate at least 3 hours if not over night.

Apple Cake
Amish Acres Kitchen

Cake:

2 1/2 c white sugar	1/2 tsp salt
1 1/4 tsp soda	2 1/4 tsp cinnamon
3 eggs	1 c vegetable oil
1 1/4 tsp vanilla	2 c wheat flour
4 c chopped apples	1 c walnuts

Mix ingredients for cake together. Pour in a 9x13 inch greased cake pan. Bake for 50 to 60 minutes. When cool, ice with cream cheese icing.

Cream Cheese Icing:

8 oz softened cream cheese	1/2 c softened butter
1 tsp vanilla	Powdered sugar
1/2 c cream	

Beat cream cheese & butter. Add vanilla & cream. Add powdered sugar until right consistency.

Bacardi Rum Cake
Bertha Hershberger

1 yellow cake mix
1 box vanilla instant pudding mix
1/2 c vegetable oil
1/2 c water
4 eggs
1/2 c rum

Grease and flour bundt pan. Mix all ingredients until smooth. Bake at 325 degrees for 1 hour. Cool in pan 25 minutes. Invert pan on plate and remove cake.

Rum Glaze:
1/2 stick butter
1/2 c sugar
1/8 c water
1/4 c rum

Melt butter, stir in water and sugar. Boil 5 minutes, stir in rum. Brush over cake. Note: If you prefer not to have such a strong rum flavor, use 1/4 c more water and omit rum. Drizzle glaze with frosting made from powdered sugar, vanilla, and milk; stir to right consistency. Refrigerate.

Chocolate Éclair Cake
Audrie Yoder-Fuchs

2 pkgs instant French vanilla pudding
3 c cold milk
Whole graham crackers
2 oz unsweetened chocolate
1 tsp vanilla
3 Tbsp milk
9 oz Cool Whip
3 Tbsp butter
2 Tbsp light Karo syrup
1 1/2 powdered sugar

Beat together pudding and milk. Fold in 9 oz Cool Whip. Prepare 9x13 inch pan with whole graham crackers. Pour in half of pudding mix. Add another layer of whole graham crackers. Pour on rest of pudding mixture. Add another layer of graham crackers.

Topping. Melt butter and unsweetened chocolate. Add Karo Syrup and 1 tsp vanilla. Blend in powdered sugar and 3 Tbsp milk. Beat until smooth and pour over all. Chill over night (8 hours).

Black Forest Cake
Theme Buffet: The Sound of Music - *Chef Brenda Ritter*

Cake:
2 - 8 oz squares dark or semisweet chocolate, room temp.
1 - 15 oz can pitted tart cherries, drained

1/3 c cherry brandy	2 Tbsp cherry brandy
2 c whipping cream	2 Tbsp half and half

1/3 c powdered sugar
18 maraschino cherries, well drained
3 - 9 inch round chocolate cake layers

Chocolate Cake Layers:

3 c cake flour	2 1/3 c sugar
1 c unsweetened cocoa powder	2 tsp baking soda
1 tsp salt	1/3 tsp baking powder
1 3/4 c milk	1 c vegetable shortening
5 eggs	1 tsp vanilla extract

Grease and flour 3 (9 inch round) cake pans. In a large bowl, sift together cake flour, sugar cocoa, baking soda, salt and baking powder. Add milk, shortening, eggs and vanilla. Using an electric mixer set at low speed, beat until well mixed, making sure all ingredients are thoroughly blended by occasionally scraping the sides of the bowl. Beat 5 more minutes on high speed. Pour one-third of the cake batter into each prepared pan. Bake 30 to 35 minutes or until a toothpick inserted in cake center comes out clean. Cool cake layers in pans on wire racks 10 minutes. Carefully remove from pans and cool completely on racks.

Coffee Cake
Ruth Ann Miller

1 box yellow cake mix	1 c and 1 Tbsp oil
1 box vanilla instant pudding	1 c water
1 box butterscotch instant pudding	4 eggs

Topping Crumbs:

1 c brown sugar	1 tsp cinnamon

Mix up batter, put half of batter in pan, then half of crumbs, then rest of batter, then remaining crumbs on top. Bake at 350 degrees for 45 minutes.

Earth Quake Cake
Enos and Katie Kuhns, grandson of M.T. Kuhns

1 c chopped pecans
German chocolate cake mix
1 stick butter

1 c shredded coconut
8 oz cream cheese
1 lb powdered sugar

Spray 12x14 inch pan. Spread pecans & coconut in pan. Prepare cake mix as instructed on box. Spread over pecans & coconut. Mix butter, cream cheese, & powdered sugar until creamy. With a spoon, dollop on top of the cake mix. No frosting needed. Bake at 350 degrees for 25 minutes.

Flower Garden Cake
Lenore Pletcher

1 Tbsp gelatine
6 egg yolks, beaten
3/4 c sugar
1 large angel food cake, broken into pieces

1/4 c cold water
3/4 c lemon juice
6 egg whites, beaten stiff

Mix gelatin and cold water and let it soak. Then mix in saucepan egg yolks, lemon juice, sugar. Then add gelatin. Cook till it coats a wooden spoon. Then in bowl mix egg whites and sugar. Beat. Then fold in egg white mixture in to saucepan. Put layers of cake and pudding into angel food cake pan and refrigerate over night. When ready to serve, flip over on plate and frost with Cool Whip. Keep refrigerated.

Heath Dessert
Nancy Hamman

1 German chocolate cake mix
Heath chips or crushed Heath bars

1 jar caramel topping
1 container Cool Whip

Make cake as directed on box (9x13 inch pan). Cool. Poke holes with end of wooden spoon on top. Pour Caramel topping over cake. Cover with Cool Whip. Top with Heath chips or crushed Heath bars.

Graham Streusel Cake
Nancy/Bertha Hershberger

Crumbs:

2 c graham crackers, crushed	3/4 c brown sugar
1 1/4 tsp cinnamon	3/4 c melted butter

Cake:

1 package yellow cake mix	3 eggs
1 c butter	1/3 c oil

Glaze:

1 c powdered sugar	1 Tbsp water

Pour half of batter into greased pan. Sprinkle with 1/2 of crumbs. Pour remaining batter into pan and sprinkle with remaining crumbs. Bake 45 to 50 minutes at 350 degrees. Mix glaze - add more water as needed until smooth.

Holiday Poke Cake
Bertha Hershberger

1 package white cake mix	1 c boiling water
1 - 4 oz package Jell-O	Cool Whip

Bake cake as directed on box. Cool. Pierce with fork at 1/2 inch intervals. Prepare Jell-O with boiling water. Pour over cooled cake. Spread with cool whip. Refrigerate.

Hungarian Coffee Cake
Audrie Yoder-Fuchs

3/4 c sugar	1 tsp cinnamon
1/2 c fine chopped nuts	1/2 c butter melted

Mix sugar, cinnamon, nuts. Shape into balls. Dip in butter and then in sugar mixture. Place in single layer of 6 balls in bottom of well greased tube pan lined with foil. Top with another layer. Cover let it rise until doubled (about 30 minutes). Bake in 350 degree oven for 35 minutes or until golden brown.

Mayonnaise Cake
Susan Nunemaker

1/2 c cocoa
1 1/2 tsp soda
1 tsp vanilla
3/4 c mayonnaise

2 c flour
1 cold water
1 c sugar

Cream together sugar & mayonnaise. Add dry ingredients to creamed mixture alternately with the cold water, beating after each addition. Add vanilla last. Bake at 350 degrees.

Mini Cheesecakes
Bertha Hershberger

12 vanilla wafers
1/2 c sugar
2 eggs

2 - 8 oz pkgs cream cheese
1 tsp vanilla

Place wafers in muffin liners. Mix other ingredients adding eggs last. Mix well and pour liners 3/4 full. Bake at 325 degrees for 25 minutes.

Praline Cheesecake
Ruth Ann Miller

1 c graham cracker crumbs
3 Tbsp oleo, melted
1 1/4 c brown sugar
3 eggs
1/2 pecans

3 Tbsp sugar
3 - 8 oz pkgs cream cheese
2 Tbsp flour
1 1/2 tsp vanilla

Combine crumbs, sugar and oleo, press onto bottom of a 9 inch pan. Bake at 350 degrees for 10 minutes. Combine cream cheese, brown sugar and flour, mix well until well blended. Blend in eggs and vanilla, stir in nuts. Pour over crust. Bake at 450 for 10 minutes. Reduce oven temperature to 250 degrees and continue baking for 30 minutes. Cool. Brush with maple syrup and garnish with pecans.

New York Cheesecake
Theme Buffet: Hello, Dolly! - *Chef Brenda Ritter*

1/2 c graham crumbs
2 Tbsp cornstarch
2 tsp vanilla
5 - 8 oz packages cream cheese, softened

1 c sugar
2 large eggs at room temp
1/2 c heavy cream

Grease 8 inch spring foam pan. Sprinkle bottom with graham cracker crumbs. In large bowl mix sugar, cornstarch and add cream cheese. Beat with mixer on medium until smooth. Beat in eggs and vanilla. Reduce to low speed and add cream, blend well. Pour in prepared pan. Bake one hour at 350 degrees.

Topping:
1/3 apricot preserves
2 peaches cut in wedges

3/4 c fresh blueberries

Melt preserves in saucepan. Press through a fine strainer. Let cool. Put blueberries in center of cheesecake, peaches around the edges then brush with preserves.

Strawberry Cake
Shirley Pitney

1 box white cake mix
1/2 c vegetable oil
1 - 10 oz box frozen strawberries

1 box dry strawberry Jell-O
1/2 c water
4 eggs

Mix together white cake mix and strawberry Jell-O. Add vegetable oil and water. Add 4 eggs one at a time. Add 1/2 of 10 oz box of frozen strawberries and juice which have thawed. Bake in 3 layers at 350 degrees for 40 minutes (Grease and flour pans.)

Icing
1 stick butter (softened - not melted)   1 box powdered sugar
Remainder of strawberries and juice.

Beat until very smooth and creamy.

Old Fashion Pineapple Upside Down Cake
Theme Buffet: Big River - *Chef Brenda Ritter*

4 eggs	1/2 c butter
1 c packed light brown sugar	1 c sifted cake flour
1 - 20 oz can pineapple slices, drained	1 tsp baking powder
10 maraschino cherries, halved	1/4 tsp salt
1 c white sugar	1 Tbsp butter, melted
1 tsp almond extract	

In a heavy skillet, melt 1/2 c butter over very low heat. Remove from heat and sprinkle brown sugar evenly over pan. Arrange pineapple slices to cover bottom of skillet. Distribute cherries around pineapple, set aside. Sift together flour, baking powder and salt. Separate the eggs into two bowls. In a large bowl, beat egg whites just until soft peaks form. Add granulated sugar gradually, beating well after each addition. Beat until stiff peaks form. In small bowl beat egg yolks at high speed until very thick and yellow. With a wire whisk or rubber scraper, using an over & under motion, gently fold egg yolks and flour mixture into whites until blended. Fold 1 Tbsp melted butter and almond extract. Spread batter evenly over pineapple in skillet. Bake for 30 to 35 minutes or until surface springs back when gently pressed with fingertip. Loosen the edges with table knife. Cool the cake for 5 minutes before inverting onto serving plate.

Royal Chocolate Sauce
Gloria Fimbianti

1/2 c light corn syrup	1 c sugar
1 c water	3 - 1 oz squares chocolate
1 tsp vanilla	1 c evaporated milk

Combine corn syrup, sugar and water. Cook to soft ball stage. Remove from heat; add chocolate squares and stir until chocolate melts. Add vanilla. Slowly add evaporated milk. Mix thoroughly. Cool. Heat over hot water to warm.

Red Velvet Cake
Bertha Hershberger

Cake:

1/2 c shortening	1 1/2 c sugar
2 eggs	2 oz red food coloring
1 tsp salt	1 c buttermilk
2 1/4 c all purpose flour	1 tsp soda
1 Tbsp vinegar	2 tsp cocoa
1 tsp vanilla	

Mix soda and vinegar in cup and let set. Cream sugar and shortenin Add eggs and mix. Add cocoa and food coloring. Alternately add sal buttermilk and flour. Stir in vanilla. Stir in soda and vinegar (add last). Bake at 350 degrees for 20 to 30 minutes. Makes 2 to 3, 9 inch (round) layers.

Frosting:

1/2 c milk	1 1/2 Tbsp flour
1/2 c sugar	1/2 c butter
1/2 tsp vanilla	Powdered sugar

Cook milk and flour in sauce pan until thick, then cool. In bowl cream sugar and butter, beat till creamy. Add vanilla, mix in cooled flour mixture and add powdered sugar until spreadable. Spread between layers and on top of cake.

Plain Ole Vanilla Wedding Cake
Rhoda Hershberger

800 lbs sugar	75 gal butter
25 c vanilla	600 lbs sifted cake flour
21 1/2 lbs baking powder	94 gal milk
7200 stiffly beaten egg whites	

Cream sugar, butter and vanilla together in bathtub. Stir together flour and baking powder in separate tub. Find a larger container, pe haps an unused grain silo; add cake flour to creamed mixture alter nately adding milk. Fold in egg whites. Pour into as many number 1 wash tubs as you can find, making all layers about the same size. Cover wash tubs and place in building that will take 28-30 minutes burn down. Remove from debris. Frost with white icing using relati ly new rowboat oars.

Scrumptious Coffee Cake
Bertha Hershberger

Cake:

2 c flour	1 tsp baking powder
1 tsp baking soda	1/4 tsp nutmeg
1 c sugar	1/2 tsp salt
1 tsp cinnamon	1/4 c orange juice
1 c milk	1 egg
1/2 c oil	

Crumbs:

1 c brown sugar	4 Tbsp margarine

Drizzle:

3/4 c powdered sugar	1/2 tsp vanilla
1 Tbsp milk	

Mix flour, baking powder, soda, nutmeg, sugar, salt, cinnamon. Mix in orange juice, milk, egg and oil. Mix just until blended. Pour into greased 9x13 inch pan. Mix together crumbs and sprinkle on top. Bake 30 minutes at 350 degrees. When cool drizzle with glaze.

Turtle Cheesecake
Mrs. Daniel (Laurie) Kuhns

1 1/2 c graham cracker crumbs	6 Tbsp margarine or butter
2 envelopes unflavored gelatin	2 - 8 oz pkgs cream cheese
2 c cottage cheese	1 c sugar
1 1/2 tsp vanilla	1/4 c caramel topping
1/4 c hot fudge topping	1/4 c pecans
8 oz container whipped topping	

Preheat oven to 350 degrees. Spray bottom & sides of 9 inch spring form pan. Melt margarine & stir in graham cracker crumbs. Press crumb mixture onto bottom & sides of pan. Bake 10 minutes. Cool. Place 1/2 cup cold water in small saucepan; sprinkle gelatin over water. Let stand 3 minutes to soften. Heat gelatin mixture over low heat until completely dissolved, stirring constantly. Combine cream cheese, cottage cheese, sugar, & vanilla in blender & blend until smooth or use wire whisk. Add gelatin mixture. Blend well. Fold in whipped topping. Pour into prepared crust. Refrigerate 4 hours, or until set. Loosen cake from sides of pan. Drizzle Caramel & hot fudge toppings over cake. Sprinkle pecans evenly over top of cake before serving.

Ultimate Chocolate Cake
Gloria Fimbianti

1/2 c butter
1 c sour cream
2 1/2 c cake flour
1 tsp vanilla
1/4 tsp salt

2 c sugar
1/2 c cocoa
1 c boiling water
2 eggs
2 tsp baking soda

Sift flour, salt and soda four times. Cream butter and sugar until light. Add well beaten egg, one at a time. Sift cocoa and add to mixture. Beat well. Add sour cream alternately with flour mixture. Add vanilla. Add boiling water. Batter will be thin. Pour into lightly greased 9x13 inch pan.

Frosting:
3 c confectioners sugar
3 Tbsp butter
1 tsp vanilla

3 Tbsp cocoa
1/4 c milk

Melt butter and milk in microwave. Add to confectioners sugar. Add vanilla. Beat until smooth. Add more milk if too thick.

Desserts
Cookies

Sugar Cookies
Amish Acres Bakery

2 c oleo
3 c white sugar
4 eggs
2 c buttermilk
2 Tbsp vanilla

1/2 tsp salt
2 tsp baking soda
6 tsp baking powder
6 c flour

Cream oleo & sugar. Add beaten eggs & milk. Mix dry ingredients. Drop by teaspoon. Press down with glass dipped in sugar. Bake at 350 degrees for 12 to 15 minutes.

Chocolate Chip Cookies
Amish Acres Bakery

2 1/2 c brown sugar
2 1/2 c white sugar
4 c oleo or butter
8 eggs
1 Tbsp water

4 tsp baking soda
10 c flour
5 c chocolate chips
1 tsp vanilla

Cream butter & sugars. Add eggs & water. Mix in rest of ingredients. Bake at 350 degrees for 10 to 12 minutes. Do not overbake.

Peanut Butter Cookies
Amish Acres Bakery

1 1/2 c oleo
2 c peanut butter
2 c white sugar
2 c brown sugar
4 eggs, beaten

4 tsp vanilla
5 c flour
1 tsp salt
3 tsp baking soda
2 tsp baking powder

Cream oleo, peanut butter, & sugars. Add egg. Mix well. Add rest of ingredients. Form balls the size of a walnut. Bake at 375 degrees for 10 to 12 minutes.

Whoopie Pies
Amish Acres Bakery

1 1/2 c oleo
3 c sugar
3 eggs
1 1/2 c sour milk
3 tsp vanilla

1 1/4 c cocoa
6 c flour
3 tsp baking soda
3 tsp salt
1 1/2 c hot water

Cream oleo & sugar. Add well beaten eggs, sour milk, vanilla, flour, cocoa, & salt. Dissolve soda in hot water & add to mixture. Drop by teaspoon on cookie sheets. Bake at 350 degrees for 10 to 12 minutes.

Filling:
3 eggs whites
3 tsp vanilla
6 Tbsp milk

1 1/2 c Crisco
3 c powdered sugar

Beat egg whites until stiff. Add vanilla, milk, & powdered sugar. Cream crisco & add to mixture. Put filling between 2 cookies.

Monster Cookies
Amish Acres Bakery

1 1/2 stick oleo
1 c white sugar
1 c brown sugar
4 eggs
1 lb peanut butter

2 1/2 tsp baking soda
4 c oatmeal (half can be flour)
1/2 lb M&M's
1 - 12 oz pkg chocolate chips

Cream sugars & oleo. Add eggs one at a time then add rest of ingredients. Add more oatmeal if necessary to make stiff dough. Form teaspoon size balls. Bake at 350 degrees for 10 minutes. Do not overbake.

Buttermilk Cookies
Amish Acres Bakery

4 c white sugar
4 c brown sugar
3 c oleo
3 c buttermilk
12 eggs, beaten

8 tsp baking soda
8 tsp baking powder
2 tsp salt
1 tsp vanilla
14 c flour

Cream sugars & oleo. Add eggs & buttermilk. Mix in rest of ingredients. Drop by teaspoon on cookie sheet. Bake at 350 degrees for 10 to 13 minutes.

Icing:
1 lb powdered sugar
2 Tbsp oleo
1/2 c milk

1 /2 c butter flavored Crisco
1/2 tsp salt
1 tsp vanilla

Mix all ingredients together, adding powdered sugar last.
Mix well & ice cookies when they have cooled.

Applesauce Spice Bars
Bertha Hershberger

Bars
1 c flour
1 tsp pumpkin pie spice
1/2 c raisins
1/2 tsp salt
1/4 c shortening

1 tsp soda
1 egg
2/3 c brown sugar
1 c applesauce

Bars: Mix all ingredients, pour into greased 9x13 inch pan.
Bake at 350 degrees for 25 minutes.

Icing
3 Tbsp butter
1 tsp vanilla

1 1/2 c powdered sugar
1 Tbsp milk

Icing: brown butter and add remaining ingredients.
Beat until smooth.

Brown Sugar Cookies
Mrs. Menno Lambright, grandson of M.T. Kuhns

5 c brown sugar
3 c slightly melted lard or oleo
3 c sweet milk or buttermilk
1 Tbsp vanilla
16 c flour (approx.)

5 beaten eggs
3 tsp soda
6 tsp baking powder
1 Tbsp lemon

Mix together and drop cookies on baking sheets.
Bake at 350 degrees.

Brownies
Gloria Fimbianti

1/2 lb margarine
4 Sqs. bakers chocolate (unsweetened)
1 tsp salt
2 c flour
1 c walnuts, cut-up

2 c sugar
4 eggs
1 tsp baking powder
2 tsp vanilla

Melt margarine and chocolate squares in microwave. Cool. In large bowl beat eggs. Add sugar & salt. Mix well. Add cooled chocolate mixture. Add flour and baking powder. Mix well. Stir in vanilla and nuts. Spread in a 15x10 inch baking sheet with sides. Bake 17 to 20 minutes. Frost with chocolate frosting. Cut into bars.

Chat & Chew Bars
Brenda Borkholder

4 c oatmeal
c brown sugar
1/2 c honey or corn syrup
tsp salt

1 1/2 c chopped nuts
3/4 c melted butter
1 tsp vanilla

Combine all ingredients. Mix well. Press firmly into well-greased jelly roll pan. Bake at 400 degrees about 10 to 12 minutes or until golden brown and bubbly. Cool thoroughly. Cut into bars.

143

Caramel Cream Sandwiches Cookies
Vernon Mishler, great-great-grandchild of M.T. Kuhns

1 c butter
1 egg yolk

3/4 c brown sugar
2 1/4 c flour

Cream together butter & brown sugar, Blend in egg yolk & flour. Chill. Shape into balls smaller then walnuts. Place on cookie sheet flatten up 1/8 inch thick, press with fork to make a design. Bake at 325 degrees till cookies turn light brown. Put 2 cookies together with frosting between them.

Frosting:
2 Tbsp butter
1/2 tsp vanilla

1 1/4 c powdered sugar
4 to 5 tsp cream

Brown butter slightly in saucepan. Remove from heat & blend in powdered sugar, vanilla, & cream. Stir until spreading consistency.

Cheese Bars
Ruth Ann Miller

2 package crescent rolls
1 c sugar
1 tsp vanilla
1/4 c sugar

2 - 8 oz pkgs cream cheese
1 egg, beaten
1 c flour
1/4 c butter, softened

Put 1 pkg crescent rolls in bottom of a greased 9x13 inch pan. Mix together the softened cream cheese, sugar, beaten egg and vanilla. Spread over crescent rolls on top of cream mixture. Crumb together sugar, flour and butter. Sprinkle on top and bake at 400 degrees for 10 minutes then at 375 degrees for 20 minutes. After this has cooled sprinkle with powdered sugar.

Chewy Oatmeal Bars
Lyle Harberger, great-great-grandson of M.T. Kuhns

1 c butter	2 c brown sugar
2 eggs	1 tsp salt
1/2 tsp vanilla	1 tsp soda
2 c flour	2 c quick oats
1/2 c peanuts	6 oz chocolate chips

Grease 15 1/2x10 1/2 inch pan. Cream butter, sugar, eggs and vanilla together until fluffy. Stir in flour, soda and salt. Add oats and mix well. Spread in pan. Sprinkle nuts and chocolate chips on top. Bake 10 minutes at 400 degrees. Do not over bake. Can add mini M&M's to top for color.

Chewy Oatmeal Cookies
Mrs. Lamar Miller, great-grandson of M.T. Kuhns

3 tsp cinnamon	2 1/4 tsp soda
1 1/2 tsp salt	3/4 tsp nutmeg
2 1/4 c oleo	3 tsp vanilla
6 eggs, beaten	6 c quick oats
3 c raisins	4 1/2 c brown sugar
4 c flour	

Cream oleo and sugar, add vanilla and eggs. Add dry ingredients, then oats and raisins. Bake at 350 degrees.

Filling
2 egg whites, beaten	2 c powdered sugar
1 1/2 c Crisco	

For filling beat powdered sugar and eggs together, add Crisco. Spread between two cookies.

Chewy Rolo Cookie Bars
Greg and Marsolie Kuhns, great-grandson of M.T. Kuhns

1 - 18.25 oz yellow cake mix   1/2 c chopped nuts
2/3 c evaporated milk   1 stick melted butter
36 Rolos cut in half (I have used bite sized Snickers too)

Preheat oven to 350 degrees & grease a 13x9 inch pan. Combine cake nix & nuts. Stir in milk & butter. Spread half of mixture into pan. Bake for 15 minutes. Remove & place Rolos cut side down on baked dough. Top with remaining cake batter. Bake at 25 to 30 minutes or until lightly brown. Cool & cut into squares.

Chocolate Chip Cookies
Jacob and Loretta Kuhns, great-grandson of M.T. Kuhns

2 1/2 c butter or oleo   3/4 c white sugar
2 1/4 c brown sugar   6 eggs
3 tsp baking soda   1 package chocolate chips
3 tsp vanilla   6 3/4 c flour
3 small boxes instant vanilla pudding

Bake at 350 degrees. Makes a good fix-n-mix bowl.

Chocolate Chip Cookies
Miriam Schrock, great-granddaughter of M.T. Kuhns

4 eggs   3 c lard or oleo
4 c brown sugar   1 c sugar
3 c milk   6 tsp baking soda
6 tsp baking powder   1 c chocolate chips
2 tsp salt   12 c flour

Mix lard, sugar, & eggs till smooth. Alternately add milk & rest of ingredients. Best if stirred very well after adding each ingredient.

Chocolate Chip Pudding Cookie
Mary Rader

2 1/4 c unsifted all-purpose flour   1 tsp baking soda
1 c butter or margarine, softened   1/4 c granulated sugar
3/4 c brown sugar, firmly packed   1 tsp vanilla
1 - 4 oz pkg Jell-O, chocolate or vanilla flavor instant pudding & pie filling
2 eggs   1 - 12 oz pkg chocolate chips
1 c chopped nuts, optional

Mix flour with baking soda. Combine butter, the sugars, pudding mix and vanilla in large mixing bowl, beat until smooth and creamy. Beat in eggs. Gradually add flour mixture; then stir in chips and nuts. (Batter will be stiff). Drop by rounded measuring teaspoonfuls onto ungreased baking sheets, about 2 inches apart. Bake at 375 for 8 to 10 minutes. Makes about 7 dozen. In high altitude areas, use large eggs; bake 9 to 11 minutes.

Coconut Cookies
Ruth Ann Miller

1 c white sugar   1 c brown sugar
1 c vegetable oil   1 c soft margarine
1 egg   2 tsp vanilla
1/2 tsp coconut flavoring   1/2 tsp black walnut flavoring
3 1/2 c flour   1 tsp cream of tartar
1/2 tsp salt   1 tsp baking soda
2 c rice crispies cereal   1 cup pecans, chopped
1 c coconut   1 c oatmeal

Mix first 8 ingredients and beat flour, cream of tartar, soda and salt. Mix well. Add cereal, oatmeal, coconut and pecans. Shape into balls. Dip fork into sugar and flatten cookie. Bake at 375 for 10 minutes.

Cowboy Cookies
Miriam Mishler, great-granddaughter of M.T. Kuhns

2 1/3 c flour	2 c brown sugar
1/2 tsp salt	2/3 c shortening
2 tsp baking powder	1/2 tsp cinnamon
1/2 tsp nutmeg	1/2 tsp soda
1 c milk	2 eggs, well beaten

Measure first 4 ingredients, work to fine crumbs. Remove 1/2 c of crumb mixture and reserve to sprinkle over top of cake. To remaining crumbs add the rest of the ingredients and beat until smooth. Bake at 375 degrees for 15 to 20 minutes.

Death by Chocolate Cookies
Andrea Stahly

2 pkgs (16 squares) bakers semi-sweet baking chocolate, divided

1/4 c firmly packed brown sugar	1/4 c margarine
2 eggs	1 tsp vanilla
1/2 c flour	1/4 tsp baking powder
2 c chopped nuts	

Heat oven to 350 degrees. Coarsely chop 8 squares of the chocolate; set aside. Microwave the remaining 8 squares chocolate in a large microwaveable bowl on 1 to 2 minutes. Stir until chocolate is melted and smooth. Stir in butter, sugar, eggs and vanilla. Stir in flour and baking powder. Stir in reserved chopped chocolate and nuts. Drop by 1/4 cupful onto an ungreased cookie sheet. Bake 12 to 13 minutes or until cookies are puffed. Cool on cookie sheet 1 minute. Remove to cookie sheet.

Pudding Cookies
Susan Nunemaker

3/4 c bisquick	1 pkg instant pudding mix
1/4 c vegetable oil	1 egg

Preheat oven at 350 degrees. Mix & form in balls. Flatten & bake 8 minutes. Makes 2 1/2 to 3 dozen.

Dream Bars
Nancy Hamman

1/2 c butter   1/2 c brown sugar
1 1/2 c flour

Cream butter, brown sugar, flour. Mix well and press in 9x13 inch pan. Bake at 350 degrees for 15 minutes. Mix together ingredients for topping and pour over crust. Bake 25 to 30 minutes. Cool.

Topping:
3 eggs, beaten   1/4 c flour
1/2 tsp salt   1 1/2 c brown sugar
1 tsp baking soda   1 1/2 c coconut
1 tsp vanilla

Crème de Menthe Brownies
Nancy Hamman

1 box brownies, bake and cool   1 can vanilla frosting
1 c chocolate chips   6 Tbsp oleo
2 Tbsp green crème de menthe syrup

Bake brownies as directed on box, cool. Combine vanilla frosting and green crème de menthe syrup. Place over brownies and chill. Melt together chocolate chips and oleo. Spread over chilled cake. Return to refrigerator. Cut & Serve.

Ervin's Cookies
Ervin Mishler, great grandson of M.T. Kuhns

2 c vegetable oil   5 c brown sugar
1/2 c milk   1/4 c vanilla
4 eggs   2 c oatmeal
1 Tbsp butter flavoring   9 c all purpose flour
4 tsp salt   2 tsp soda
1 1/2 Tbsp baking powder   3 c chocolate chips

Bake at 375 degrees for 8 to 10 minutes.
Cookies will appear moist. Do not over bake.

Farmer Boy Cookies
Junita Mullett, great-granddaughter of M.T. Kuhns

2 c flour
1 tsp baking powder
2 c oatmeal
1 c coconuts or chopped nuts
1/2 c chocolate chips
1 c brown sugar
2 eggs

1 tsp soda
1 tsp salt
1 c raisins
1/2 c peanut butter
1 c soft margarine
1 c white sugar

Mix together flour, soda, baking powder and salt. Mix together oatmeal, raisins, coconut, peanut butter and chocolate chips. Mix together margarine, sugars and eggs. Mix each well, separately. Then add flour to sugar mix and last the oatmeal mix. Bake at 350 degrees for 10 minutes or until nice and brown.

Sand Art Brownies
Mark Mishler, great-great grandson of M.T. Kuhns

2/3 c cocoa
1 c chocolate chips
1 c butterscotch chips or white vanilla chips
2 1/4 c flour
2 tsp vanilla
6 eggs

1/3 c sugar
1 1/3 c brown sugar

1 c walnuts, chopped
1 1/3 c oil

Pour into greased 7x11 inch pan. Bake at 350 degrees.

Ginger Cookies
Bertha Hershberger

3/4 c shortening
1 egg, beaten
1/4 c molasses
1 tsp cinnamon
1 tsp ginger

1 c sugar
2 c and 2 Tbsp flour
2 tsp soda
1 tsp cloves

Cream together sugar and shortening. Add egg and molasses, stir. Add dry ingredients. Make into small balls; roll in dish of sugar. Bake on greased sheets at 325 degrees for 10 to 12 minutes.

Good Oatmeal Cookies

Anna B. Kauffman, granddaughter of M.T. Kuhns

1 1/2 c flour
1 tsp baking powder
1 tsp vanilla
1 c shortening
3 c quick oats

1/2 tsp salt
1 tsp baking soda
2 c brown sugar
2 eggs

Cream shortening and sugar, add eggs and vanilla. Add dry ingredients. Form into balls, roll in powdered sugar. Bake at 350 degrees.

Grandma's Cookies

Sovilla Kuhns

2 c brown sugar
1 c lard
1 tsp baking soda
Enough flour to make a nice dough - not too stiff

2 eggs
1 c buttermilk
2 tsp baking powder

Cream lard & brown sugar, add eggs, buttermilk & dry ingredients. Drop on greased baking sheet. Bake in moderate oven.

Irresistible Peanut Butter Cookies

Mrs. Glen Harshberger

3/4 c peanut butter
1 1/4 c brown sugar
1 Tbsp vanilla
1 3/4 c flour
3/4 tsp soda

1/2 c shortening
3 Tbsp milk
1 egg
3/4 tsp salt

Combine peanut butter, shortening, brown sugar, milk, & vanilla. Beat until well blended. Beat egg into peanut butter mixture. Combine flour, slat, & soda. Add to creamed mixture. Mix until just blended. Drop by tablespoon on ungreased cookie pans. Bake at 375 degrees for 7 to 8 minutes. Cool for 2 minutes on baking sheet. Then place on wire rack to cool.

Just Right Chocolate Chip Cookies
Brenda Borkholder

2/3 c oleo	2/3 c butter flavored Crisco
1 tsp baking soda	1/2 tsp salt
1 box instant pudding	3 1/4 c Robin Hood flour
3/4 c white sugar	3/4 c brown sugar
1 1/2 tsp vanilla	2 eggs
1 tsp butternut flavorings	1 - 12 oz pkg chocolate chips

Bake at 375 degrees for 8 to 10 minutes.

Lemon Bars
Leon Kuhns, great-grandson of M.T. Kuhns

2 c flour	1/2 c melted oleo
1/2 c powdered sugar	4 eggs
2 c sugar	1/2 c flour
1/2 c lemon juice	

Combine first 3 ingredients and press into greased and floured 9x13 inch pan. Bake for 15 to 20 minutes at 350 degrees. Combine rest of ingredients and pour over baked crust. Bake additional 25 minutes. When done dust with powdered sugar.

No Bake Granola Bars
Omer and Barbara Kuhns, great-grandson of M.T. Kuhns

1/2 c brown sugar	1/2 c light corn syrup
1 c peanut butter	1 tsp vanilla
1 1/2 c Rice Krispies	1 c raisins
1/2 c coconut	2 Tbsp sesame seeds
1 1/2 c oatmeal	

Mix and bring to a boil the brown sugar and syrup. Stir in peanut butter and vanilla. Add dry ingredients. Press into 9x13 inch pan. Cut into bars when cooled.

Lemon Cheese Bars
Bertha Hershberger

Bars

1 box yellow cake mix
1 - 8 oz pkg cream cheese
1/3 c sugar
1/2 c coconut

2 eggs, divided
1/3 c oil
2 tsp lemon juice
1 c chopped nuts

Mix cake mix, egg and oil until crumbly; reserve 1 c mixture for topping. Pat remaining crumb mixture into ungreased 9x13 inch pan. Bake for 15 minutes at 350 degrees. Beat together cream cheese, sugar, lemon juice and egg until light and smooth. Spread over partially baked layer. Sprinkle with nuts, coconut and reserved crumbs. Bake 15 minutes longer. Cool and drizzle with glaze.

Glaze:

1 c powdered sugar
1/4 tsp lemon juice

2 Tbsp water

Mix all ingredients together and drizzle on top of cake.

Little Debbie Cookies
Mrs. Noah Kuhns, grandson of M.T. Kuhns

1 c oleo
4 eggs
1 1/2 tsp nutmeg
3 c flour

2 c brown sugar
2 tsp cinnamon
1 tsp baking soda
3 c oatmeal

Cream oleo, sugar, eggs, cinnamon, & nutmeg. Then add rest of ingredients. Roll in small balls and flatten on cookie sheet. Bake at 350 degrees. Fill with filling.

Filling:

2 egg whites
4 Tbls milk
1 c Crisco

2 tsp vanilla
4 c powdered sugar

Beat eggs whites then add vanilla, milk, & 2 cups powdered sugar. Beat thoroughly then add rest of powdered sugar & Crisco.

Luscious Lemon Bars
Ruth Ann Miller

Crust
1 c oleo
2 c flour

Dash of salt
1/2 c powdered sugar

Filling
4 eggs
6 Tbsp lemon juice

2 c white sugar
1/4 c flour

Mix well oleo, salt, flour and powdered sugar. Pat into a 13x9 inch pan. Bake at 350 degrees for 15 minutes or until done. Cool slightly. Beat eggs, sugar, lemon juice and flour. Pour over slightly cooled crust. Bake at 350 degrees for 25 minutes or till set. Cool. Sprinkle with powdered sugar.

Merry Christmas Sugar Cookies
Bertha Hershberger

4 1/2 c flour
1 tsp soda
1 1/2 c sugar
1/3 c orange juice
1/2 tsp almond extract

1/2 tsp salt
1 c shortening
1 tsp vanilla
3 eggs

Sift flour, salt and soda together. Cream together shortening, sugar, vanilla, orange juice, eggs and almond extract. Mix all ingredients together. Bake at 350 degrees for 8 to 10 minutes.

Peanut Butter Cornflakes
Audrie Yoder-Fuchs

2 c sugar
10 c cornflakes (Measure uncrushed - then crush cornflakes)
2 c peanut butter

1 c dark Karo syrup

Heat sugar & syrup only until it bubbles around edge of pan and sugar is dissolved. Stir constantly. Take from stove and stir in crushed cornflakes and put in butter pan. Cool and cut. Can spread chocolate on top for variety.

Never Fail Sugar Cookies
Rhoda Hershberger

3 c sugar   2 c vegetable oil   4 eggs
Combine and beat well. Then add
2 c buttermilk with 2 tsp soda   3 tsp vanilla
6 tsp baking powder   6 c flour

Mix well. Bake at 450 degrees for 10 to 12 minutes.

Frosting: melt together 1 c brown sugar, 1 stick margarine.
Add 3 to 4 Tbsp milk and enough powdered sugar for right spreading consistency.

Oatmeal Cookies
Bertha Hershberger

1 1/2 c flour   1/2 c salt
1 tsp baking powder   1 tsp soda
2 c brown sugar   1 c shortening
2 eggs, slightly beaten   1 tsp vanilla
3 c quick oatmeal   Powdered sugar

Sift flour, salt, baking powder, soda. Cream sugar and shortening, add eggs and vanilla. Beat well. Add dry ingredients and oatmeal. Chill dough, form into balls, roll in powdered sugar until coated. Bake at 350 degrees for 8 to 10 minutes.

Oatmeal Scotchies
Linda Schrock, great-granddaughter of M.T. Kuhns

3 c butter flavored Crisco   4 1/2 c brown sugar
6 eggs   3 Tbsp water
3 tsp vanilla   6 c flour
6 tsp baking powder   3 tsp soda
2 tsp salt   4 1/2 c oatmeal
2 to 3 c butterscotch chips

Beat together Crisco and brown sugar until smooth. Add beaten eggs, water and vanilla. Sift together dry ingredients and add. Mix well. Add oatmeal and chips. Bake at 375 degrees.

Peanut Butter Bars
Ruth Ann Miller

1 1/2 c crushed graham crackers
1 lb powdered sugar
1 c chocolate chips
1 tsp peanut butter

1 c butter, softened
1 c peanut butter
1 c butterscotch chips

Cream powdered sugar and butter until smooth. Add cracker crumbs and peanut butter and stir with spoon until smooth. Press into a 9x13 inch pan. Melt chocolate chips, butterscotch chips and peanut butter together in a double broiler. Spread over bars. Cut into squares before chocolate is completely set. Refrigerate.

Peanut Butter Chocolate Chip Cookies
Mrs. Marie Schrock, great-grandchild of M.T. Kuhns

2 c shortening
2 c peanut butter
4 tsp vanilla
2 tsp baking soda
1/2 c milk

4 c sugar
4 eggs
2 tsp salt
5 c flour
4 c chocolate chips

Mix shortening, sugar, peanut butter, eggs & vanilla. Add sifted dry ingredients alternately with milk. Roll out 1/4 inch thick onto wax paper. Melt chocolate chips over hot water & cool slightly. Spread on cookie dough. Roll jelly roll fashion & chill 1/2 hour. Slice 1/8 inch thick & bake lightly.

Peanut Butter Cookies
John and Susie Kuhns, great-grandson of M.T. Kuhns

1 c sugar
1 c brown sugar
1 c peanut butter
1 tsp vanilla
2 1/2 to 3 c flour

1/2 c Crisco
2 eggs
1 package chocolate chips
2 tsp soda
1 tsp salt

Cream sugars & Crisco. Then add peanut butter & eggs. Beat well then add rest of ingredients. Roll into balls, press with fork. Bake at 350 degrees until light brown.

156

Peanut Butter Krispie Treats
Brenda Beehler

3 c crispy rice cereal   1/4 c creamy peanut butter
6 oz (3 Squares) white chocolate or vanilla almond bark

Lightly grease 8x8 inch pan. Place white chocolate and peanut butter in microwave save dish and heat for 1 minute. Continue to melt in 15 second intervals until mixture is creamy. Pour mixture over cereal and stir. Press firmly in pan and refrigerate for 30 minutes. Can top with frosting and sprinkles. For Valentines Day place in heart shaped pan, frost and decorate with candies.

Pecan Pie Bars
Mrs. Larry Miller, great-grandson of M.T. Kuhns

1 package yellow cake mix	1/2 c margarine, melted
1 egg	1 tsp vanilla
1 1/2 c corn syrup	1/2 c brown sugar
1 tsp vanilla	3 eggs
1 c chopped pecans	

Mix together cake mix, (except 2/3 c set aside) margarine, egg and vanilla. Press evenly in bottom and sides of 9x13 inch greased pan. Bake at 350 degrees for 15 to 20 minutes. Combine rest of cake mix, corn syrup, brown sugar, vanilla and eggs. Pour over baked crust. Sprinkle with chopped pecans and return to oven to bake for 30 to 35 minutes or until filling is set. Cut into bars.

Quick Saucepan Cookies
Albert Kuhns family, great-grandson of M.T. Kuhns

3 1/4 c brown sugar	1 1/4 c oil
5 eggs (add one at a time)	2 tsp vanilla
3 3/4 tsp baking powder	1 c butterscotch chips
1 c chocolate chips	4 1/4 c flour
1 1/2 c chopped nuts (optional)	

Mix sugar & oil well. Add eggs. Beat well. Add the rest of ingredients. Blend well. Bake at 350 degrees for 25 to 30 minutes in a large 11x17 inch cookie sheet. Cut into bars when warm (not hot or warm).

Pecan Tarts
Ruth Ann Miller

1/2 c butter
2 egg yolks
2 c flour
1/2 c brown sugar
2 tsp vanilla
2 Tbls melted butter

1/2 c sugar
1 tsp almond flavor
2 eggs
1 c pecans
Pinch of salt

Mix butter, sugar, egg yolks, almond flavor and flour. Press evenly into tart shells. Mix eggs, brown sugar, pecans, vanilla, salt and melted butter. Place one tsp of mixture in each shell. Bake at 350 degrees for 15 minutes. Makes 4 dozen.

Pecan Turtle Bars
Jean Chupp

2 c flour
1/2 c butter

1 c brown sugar
1 c chopped pecans

Mix flour, butter and brown sugar together and pat into 9x13 inch pan, top with pecans. In sauce pan add 2/3 c butter & 1/2 c brown sugar cook over low heat, stirring constantly until it boils 1/2 to 1 minute. Pour over pecans & crust and bake at 350 degrees for 20 minutes or till caramel layer is bubbly and crust is brown. Remove from oven and sprinkle 1 c milk chocolate chips. Allow chips to melt slightly, swirl as they melt.

Scotchies
Nancy Hamman

1 c sugar
10 cups Special K or Corn Flakes
1/2 package chocolate chips

2 c corn syrup
1/2 c peanut butter
1/2 pkg butterscotch chips

Bring sugar and syrup to a rolling boil. Add peanut butter. Pour mixture over 10 cups of Special K or Corn Flakes. Melt chocolate chips and butterscotch chips together and spread on top.

Preaching Pies
Amish Acres Kitchen

Pastry:
2 1/4 c flour
1/2 tsp salt

1/3 c shortening
1/3 c cold water

Apple Filling:
3 c diced apples
1 Tbsp flour
2 Tbsp rich milk

2/3 c sugar
1/2 tsp cinnamon or nutmeg
2 Tbsp butter (optional)

Pastry: Combine flour and salt in a mixing bowl. Cut shortening into flour with a pastry blender or two knives. Do not over mix; these are sufficiently blended when particles are the size of peas. Add water gradually, sprinkle 1 Tbsp at a time over mixture. Toss lightly with a fork until particles of flour have been dampened. Use only enough water to hold the pastry together when it is pressed between fingers. It should not feel wet. Roll dough into a round ball approximately 3 inches in diameter. Handle as little as possible. Fill with apples.

Apple Filling: Mix apples, sugar, flour and spice together until well blended. Spoon filling onto pastry circles. Fold in half, seal edge and crimp. Brush with cream and sprinkle with sugar before baking. Bake at 375 degrees for 18 to 20 minutes.

Snicker Cookies
Nancy Hamman

1/2 c sugar
1 egg
1/2 tsp soda
1/2 c peanut butter
1/2 tsp baking powder

1/2 c oleo
1 1/2 c flour
1/2 c brown sugar
1 1/2 tsp vanilla
1/2 tsp salt

Press flat in hand and press around small candy bar. Place on cookie sheet and bake at 375 degrees for 12 minutes (leave on cookie sheet 10 minutes before removing).

Pumpkin Spice Bars
Arlene Miller, great-granddaughter of M.T. Kuhns

4 eggs	2 c sugar
1 c vegetable oil	1 - 16 oz can pumpkin
2 c flour	2 tsp baking powder
2 tsp ground cinnamon	1 tsp baking soda
3/4 tsp salt	1/2 tsp ground ginger
1/4 tsp ground cloves	1/2 c raisins (optional)

Frosting:

1 - 3 oz cream cheese	1 tsp vanilla
1/4 c and 2 Tbsp margarine or butter	2 c powdered sugar

Heat oven to 350 degrees. Grease jelly roll pan,
15 1/2x10x1 1/2 inch. Beat eggs, sugar, oil, pumpkin.
Stir in flour, baking powder, cinnamon, soda, salt, ginger, & cloves.
Mix in raisins. Pour batter into pan. Bake until light brown, 25 to
30 minutes. Cool, frost with cream cheese icing. Cut into bars.
Refrigerate any remaining bars.

Pumpkin Whoopee Pie Cookies
Rhoda Hershberger

2 egg yolks	2 c brown sugar
1 c vegetable oil	1 tsp cloves (ground)
1 tsp cinnamon	1 tsp ginger
1 tsp salt	1 tsp baking powder
1 tsp soda	1 tsp vanilla
2 c mashed cooked pumpkin	3 c flour

Filling:

2 unbeaten egg whites	1 1/2 c. shortening
2 tsp vanilla	4 Tbsp flour
2 Tbsp milk	2 to 4 c powdered sugar

Beat yolks, sugar and oil together until smooth. Combine with dry
ingredients and pumpkin. Drop by teaspoons onto cookie sheet
and bake at 350 degrees for 12 minutes.

Filling: Combine all ingredients and beat to right consistency.
Spread between two cookies.

Pumpkin Bars
Rhoda Hershberger

2 c flour
2 tsp baking powder
1/2 tsp cinnamon
4 eggs, beaten
1 c mashed cooked pumpkin

2 c sugar
1 tsp soda
1/8 tsp salt
1 c vegetable oil

Cream Cheese Icing:
1 - 3 oz pkg cream cheese, softened
1 tsp vanilla
1 Tbsp milk

2 c powdered sugar
6 Tbsp butter or margarine

Combine all ingredients and mix well. Pour into greased and floured 15x10x1 inch pan. Bake at 350 degrees for 25 to 30 minutes. Combine icing ingredients and spread on cooled bars. Optional sprinkle with chopped nuts.

Sour Cream Raisin Bars
Bertha Hershberger

Crust:
1 3/4 c oatmeal
1/2 c sugar
1 c margarine
1 tsp baking powder

1 3/4 c flour
1/2 c brown sugar
1 tsp soda
Salt & vanilla

Filling:
4 egg yolks
1 c sugar
2 c raisins

2 c sour cream
1 Tbsp cornstarch

Mix and pat 3/4 of crumbs in a 9x13 inch pan. Bake 15 minutes and cool. Bring ingredients to a boil stirring often. Pour onto crust, cover with remaining crumbs. Bake 20 more minutes.

Spicy Sugar Cookies
Velda Kuhns, great-great granddaughter of M.T. Kuhns

1 1/2 c shortening
2 eggs
4 Tbsp milk
5 c sifted flour
1 1/2 tsp salt

2 c sugar
1/2 c honey or sorghum
2 tsp vanilla
3 tsp soda
2 tsp cinnamon

Cream together sugar & shortening. Blend in eggs, honey, milk and vanilla. Sift together & add to creamed mixture rest of ingredients. Make balls, dip in sugar. Bake 375 degrees, 8 to 10 minutes.

Sugar Cookies
Orva E. and Esther Miller, great-grandson of M. T. Kuhns

2 c vegetable oil
4 eggs
2 tsp baking soda
6 tsp baking powder

3 c white sugar
2 c buttermilk
6 3/4 c all-purpose flour
3 tsp vanilla

Mix sugar and oil together, then add eggs, one at a time, beating thoroughly with a wooden spoon after each addition. Mix soda into buttermilk. Mix baking powder with flour, then add flour and milk alternately into sugar and egg mixture. Add vanilla and beat. Drop onto Teflon coated cookie sheet and bake at 350 degrees. Makes 6 to 8 dozen.

Chocolate Chip Cookies
Angie Pletcher-Stillson

1/2 c shortening
2 1/2 c flour
1/2 cup sugar
1 tsp vanilla
1 - 12 oz package semisweet chocolate chips

1/2 c margarine
1 c packed brown sugar
2 eggs
1/2 tsp baking soda

In a mixing bowl beat the shortening and margarine for 30 seconds. Add half of the flour, brown sugar, sugar, eggs, vanilla and baking soda. Beat mixture till thoroughly combined. Beat in the remaining flour. Stir in chocolate chips. Drop on ungreased cookie sheet. Bake at 375 degrees for 8 to 10 minutes. Makes about 5 dozen.

Desserts

Amish Tapioca Pudding
Amish Acres Kitchen

1 - 2 lb can crushed pineapple   1 container Cool Whip
1 large can mandarin oranges, halved, drained (save juice)
6 cups liquid, including syrup drained from fruit and water
1/2 c baby pearl tapioca   1 - 3 oz orange gelatin
1 c sugar   1 pinch of salt

Drain fruit and set aside. Add water to fruit syrup to make 6 cups.
Bring to a boil and add tapioca. Boil 15 minutes. Let stand 10 minutes. Add gelatin, sugar and salt. When mixture is cool, stir in
pineapple and oranges. Let set in refrigerator. Just before serving,
stir in Cool Whip.

Apple and Blueberry Crumble
Theme Buffet: **My Fair Lady -** *Chef Brenda Ritter*

1 1/2 c flour   1 1/2 c dark brown sugar
6 oz butter, cut in small pieces   1/2 tsp cinnamon
2 Tbsp lemon juice   1 can blueberry pie filling
1 can apple pie filling

Put flour and brown sugar into mixing bowl, add butter and crumble it with your fingers, until it resembles coarse breadcrumbs. Put
blueberry and apple pie filling in soufflé dish, sprinkle with lemon
juice and cinnamon. Heap crumble mixture on top pressing it
down gently. Cover all the filling. Bake at 350 degrees for 20 minutes or until golden brown.

Apple Crisp
Mrs. Amos Borkholder, granddaughter of M.T. Kuhns

1/2 c brown sugar   1/3 c flour
1 c quick oatmeal   1/2 tsp salt
1 tsp cinnamon   1/3 c oleo
4 c sliced apples

Mix first 6 ingredients together. Put apples in bottom of pan,
put crumbs on top & bake at 375 degrees for 30 minutes.

Apple Dumplings

Mrs. Omar Kuhns, grandson of M.T. Kuhns

Dough

3 c flour
2 tsp salt
1 1/2 c milk
Brown sugar, chopped apples, cinnamon

3 tsp baking powder
3 Tbsp lard

Sauce

2 1/2 c sugar
1 tsp salt

3 Tbsp flour
2 1/2 c hot water

Mix dough ingredients roll up like cinnamon rolls, then add apples, brown sugar, & cinnamon, on top of dough. Roll & cut 1 inch thick & put in pan. Mix together sauce & boil 3 minutes.

Apple Dumplings

Mrs. Clyde Yoder, great-granddaughter of M.T. Kuhns

2 c sifted flour
2 tsp baking powder
2 unbeaten eggs

2 c sugar
1 1/2 tsp salt
2/3 c cream

Fill 9x13 inch pan with thinly sliced apples. Mix dry ingredients together, mix in eggs with hand until crumbly. Put on apple slices. On top of this pour cream and sprinkle with cinnamon. Bake at 350 degrees until nice & brown. Serve warm with milk or ice cream. Delicious.

Frozen Cherry Delight

Jacob and Loretta Kuhns, great-grandson of M.T. Kuhns

1 can cherry pie filling
1 can crushed pineapple

1 can Eagle brand milk
1-16 oz Cool Whip

Mix & pour into cake pan. Set in freezer.

Apple Enchiladas
Brenda Borkholder

21 oz can apple pie filling
1 tsp cinnamon
1 tsp vanilla
1 c brown sugar

6 - 8 inch flour tortillas
1/3 c butter
Pinch of salt
1/2 c water

Spoon pie filling evenly down center of tortilla. Sprinkle with cinnamon. Roll up and place seam side down in lightly greased 2 qt baking dish. Bring butter and vanilla, salt, sugar and water to a boil in a saucepan, reduce heat, simmer, stirring constantly for 3 to 5 minutes. Pour over enchiladas. Let stand 30 minutes. Bake at 350 degrees for 20 minutes. Serve warm.

Apple Rhubarb Crisp
Mervin Mishler, great-grandson of M.T. Kuhns

2 c apples, cut fine
2 Tbsp flour
3/4 c white sugar

2 c rhubarb, cut fine
1 egg, beaten
1/4 tsp nutmeg

Crumbs:
1/2 c butter
1 c brown sugar

1 c flour

Mix apples, rhubarb, flour, egg, white sugar and nutmeg together. Place in glass baking dish. Combine butter, flour and brown sugar to crumbly consistency. Put on top of apple-rhubarb mixture. Bake at 375 degrees for 30 minutes. Serve warm with milk.

Cherry Dessert
Elizabeth M. Schrock, granddaughter of M.T. Kuhns

1 c oatmeal
1 c brown sugar
1 can cherries (or any fruit you desire) thickened with a little cornstarch

1/2 c flour
1/2 c oleo

Mix first 4 ingredients into crumbs. Put half of crumbs into bottom of pan. Put fruit on top then rest of crumbs on top.

Baklava
Theme Buffet: Zorba - *Chef Brenda Ritter*

1 package filo dough
1 lb sugar
3 cinnamon sticks

2 to 3 lbs crushed walnuts
5 to 6 c water
1 lb melted butter

Unroll filo dough. Butter sides and bottom of 9x12 inch baking dish. Carefully lift one piece of dough off and place gently into dish. Brush with melted butter. Generously sprinkle with crushed walnuts. Repeat until all dough is layered with nuts. When finished cut on a diagonal line to form triangles, refrigerate.
Syrup: Combine in medium saucepan water, sugar and cinnamon sticks. Bring to a rolling boil, making sure to stir to prevent sticking. Remove Baklava from refrigerator making sure it is cold, pour hot sauce over top. Saturate thoroughly. Bake at 350 degrees until golden brown, about 30 minutes. Cool and serve.

Banana Split Dessert
Ruth Ann Miller

2 pkg graham crackers, crushed
1/2 c powdered sugar
2 eggs
1 tsp vanilla
Sliced bananas

3/4 stick butter, melted
1/2 c oleo
2 c powdered sugar
10 oz jar of Cool Whip

Crush graham crackers, add melted butter and powdered sugar. Mix well and put in bottom of loaf pan. Mix oleo, eggs, powdered sugar and vanilla. Beat at high speed for 5 minutes. Put this on top of cracker crust. Put Cool Whip on top of pudding. Slice bananas on top of Cool Whip.

Frank Butler's Butterfingers
Theme Buffet: Annie Get Your Gun - *Chef Brenda Ritter*

2 1/4 c graham cracker crumbs
1/2 lb   melted butter

1 1/2 c peanut butter
12 oz pkg chocolate morsels

Mix all except morsels together and spread out onto a cookie sheet (12x24x1). Melt morsels and spread over top. Cut immediately, chill for 3 hours. Serve.

Better than Robert Redford
Nancy Hamman

Crust:
1 c flour
1 stick oleo   1 Tbsp sugar

Layer 1:
18 oz package cream cheese, soft   1 c powdered sugar
2 c Cool Whip

Layer 2:
2 pkg instant pudding (chocolate, vanilla, banana, butterscotch)
3 c milk

Mix ingredients for crust, press into 9x13 inch pan. Bake at 350 degrees for 20 minutes. Mix ingredients for Layer 1. Spread over crust. Mix ingredients for Layer 2 pour over Layer 1. Chill. Top with Cool Whip.

Brownies
Ruth Ann Miller

2/3 c Crisco   1/2 c cocoa
2 c sugar   4 eggs
1 1/2 c flour   1 tsp salt
1 tsp baking powder   1 c nuts (optional)
1 pint jar of marshmallow cream   1 c brown sugar
1/2 c cocoa   1/3 c water
1/3 c butter

Melt Crisco with cocoa over low heat. Add sugar, eggs, and beat together. Sift flour, salt, and baking powder. Add to first mixture with nuts. Spread in greased 9x13 inch pan. Bake 30 minutes at 350 or until done. Cool a minute. Then spread 1 pint jar of marshmallow cream. Bring remaining ingredients to boil for 3 minutes (brown sugar, cocoa, water and butter). Let cool, add powdered sugar until thick enough to spread. Spread over marshmallow cream.

Burnt Trinity College Raspberry Creams
Theme Buffet: My Fair Lady - Chef Brenda Ritter

5 egg yolks
2 c heavy cream
Fresh raspberries

1 c plus 2 Tbsp sugar
1/2 tsp vanilla

Beat yolks with 2 Tbsp sugar for 3 minutes with mixer. Add cream and continue to beat until mixture is thick and creamy. Transfer to sauce pan, add vanilla. Bring to almost a boil, stirring constantly. Pour into shallow baking dish. Let cool to room temperature. Add fresh raspberries over top. Cool in refrigerator for at least 2 hours. Just before serving, sprinkle with remaining sugar, put under very hot broiler so that sugar caramelizes to a deep glaze.

Caramel Tapioca
Mrs. Jerry Miller, great-granddaughter of M.T. Kuhns

6 c boiling water
1 tsp salt
2 eggs
1 c milk
Whipped cream, whipped
Bananas and Milky Way candy bars, cut up

1 1/2 c tapioca
2 c brown sugar
1 1/2 c white sugar
1 stick butter

Cook water, tapioca, & salt for 15 minutes. Add brown sugar & cook until done. Mix together eggs, milk, & sugar. Add this to tapioca mixture. Cook until it bubbles. Brown butter & add 1 tsp vanilla. Cool & add whipped cream, bananas & candy bars.

Chocolate Bavarian Cream
Theme Buffet: Triumph of Love - Chef Brenda Ritter

2 oz chocolate
6 Tbsp dry cocoa powder
1/2 c milk, scalded
1/8 tsp salt
2 tsp vanilla

2 packages unflavored gelatin
2 Tbsp water
1/2 c sugar
2 c heavy cream

Soak gelatin in cold water and dissolve in hot milk. Add chocolate and cocoa powder and stir until smooth. Whip cream until stiff and fold in. Chill 2 hours.

169

Cherry and Blueberry Cobbler
Theme Buffet: Annie Get Your Gun - *Chef Brenda Ritter*

1 oz baking powder
2 eggs
1 tsp salt
8 oz butter
Fresh cherries and blueberries

1 tsp cinnamon
7 oz sugar
1 c milk
1 cap full vanilla extract
12 oz flour

Streusel:
6 oz brown sugar
6 oz butter
20 oz cake flour

3 oz sugar
1/2 tsp cinnamon

Place the flour, baking powder, salt, sugar and cinnamon in a bowl and mix. Slowly add the eggs and the other wet ingredients. Melt the butter and add. Pour mixture over berries in a deep ramekin and bake at 375 degrees. Streusel topping can be mixed together and added on top before baking.

Cherry Tartlets
Gloria Fimbianti

1 1/4 c flour
1/4 tsp salt
2 egg yolks
1 can prepared cherry pie filling
1 - 3 oz package cream cheese
1 Tbsp milk

1/4 c sugar
1/2 c butter
1 tsp vanilla
1/4 tsp almond extract
1/4 c sifted powdered sugar

Sift flour, sugar and salt. Cut in butter. Add egg yolks and vanilla. Mix until soft dough is formed. Press into buttered mini muffin tins. Bake. Cool. Remove from tins. Add almond extract to cherry pie filling. Blend cream cheese with powdered sugar and milk. Spread over bottom of tartlet. Chill, arrange cherries on top. Chill.

Chocolate Brownie Dessert
Jeff Dorsey

1 box brownies (any variety)   4 Heath candy bars, crushed
1 small box instant chocolate pudding
1 small container Cool Whip

Bake 13x9 inch pan of brownies as directed on box and cool. Make pudding as directed on box and refrigerate. After brownies are cool crumble 1/2 the brownies on bottom of a large serving bowl. Spread a layer of pudding on top, then a layer of Cool Whip. Sprinkle 1/2 the crushed candy bars on top. Repeat layers. Cover & refrigerate. *Can substitute chocolate pudding for butterscotch and Heath Bar for Butterfinger.

Chocolate Crunch Brownies
Treva Miller, great-granddaughter of M.T. Kuhns

1 c butter   2 c sugar
4 eggs   6 Tbsp cocoa
1 c flour   2 tsp vanilla
1/2 tsp salt   1 - 8 oz marshmallow cream
1 c peanut butter   2 c chocolate chips
3 c crisp rice cereal

In mixing bowl cream butter and sugar, add eggs. Stir in cocoa, flour, vanilla and salt. Pour into a greased 13x9 inch baking pan. Bake at 350 degrees for 25 minutes. Cool. Spread marshmallow cream over cooled brownies. In small saucepan melt peanut butter and chocolate chips over low heat, stirring constantly. Remove from heat and stir in cereal. Spread over marshmallow layer.

Delicious Homemade Ice Cream
Velda Kuhns, great-great granddaughter of M.T. Kuhns

3 eggs   1 c sugar
1 box instant vanilla pudding 1 1/2 c whipped cream
Pinch of salt   1 Tbsp vanilla
3 c milk, scalded
3 1/2 c marshmallows, melted in 2 cups milk
Use 1 gallon ice cream & freeze.

eserts

Chocolate Topiary Raspberry Shrub
Theme Buffet: Triumph of Love - *Chef Brenda Ritter*

12 cream puffs
6 chocolate covered pretzel sticks
Ganache

1/2 c fresh raspberries
2 oz chocolate chips
6 coupe glasses

Melt chocolate chips. Place small amount in center of each glass. Stick one pretzel in each glass. Place two cream puffs topiary fashion on pretzels. Pour ganache over puffs. Add fresh raspberries around glass. Dollop whip cream on top.

Ganache:
2 lbs chocolate
2 oz butter

1 qt heavy cream

Heat cream almost to a boil, add butter and chocolate, stir until completely smooth

Cinnamon Pudding
LaVern and Lenore Pletcher

2 c brown sugar
2 Tbsp butter
2 tsp baking powder
1 c milk
1/2 tsp salt

1 1/2 c cold water
2 scant c flour
1 c sugar
2 tsp cinnamon
2 Tbsp butter

Combine brown sugar, cold water and butter, bring to boil (will make a syrup). Combine flour, baking powder, sugar, milk, cinnamon, salt and butter. Put in greased oblong pan. Put syrup on top of dough and sprinkle with nuts, if desired. Bake at 350 degrees for 25 to 30 minutes.

Cream Puffs
Theme Buffet: Triumph of Love - *Chef Brenda Ritter*

1/2 c shortening
1 c boiling water
3 eggs, unbeaten

1/8 tsp salt
1 c sifted flour

Add shortening and salt to boiling water and stir over medium heat until boiling again. Lower heat and add flour all at once. Stir vigorously until mixture leaves sides of pan. Remove from heat, add one egg at a time, beating after each. Shape on ungreased cookie sheet using 1 teaspoon for puff. Bake at 450 degrees for 20 minutes then reduce heat to 350 degrees for additional 20 minutes. Remove from oven and place on rack to cool. When cool, make a slit on each side of puff and fill with cream filling.

Filling:
1/3 c sugar
1/4 tsp salt
2 c milk, scalded
1 tsp vanilla

3 Tbsp corn starch
2 egg yolks
2 Tbsp butter

Combine sugar, corn starch and salt very thoroughly, add egg yolks and beat well. Add a little bit of the milk. Slowly mix and return mixture to rest of hot milk. Cook over boiling water, stirring constantly until mixture thickens. Add butter, cool and add vanilla. Put in pastry bag when completely cool and fill cream puffs.

Crème Caramele
Theme Buffet: Zorba - *Chef Brenda Ritter*

10 eggs, separated
1 c sugar

1 1/4 qt heavy cream
1 tsp vanilla

Put heavy cream in pot. Add 1/2 cup sugar, bring almost to boil. Beat egg yolks with 1/2 c sugar. Add 1 c cream mixture to egg yolks to temper. Then add rest of cream and vanilla. Mix well, pour into custard cups, put in baking pan and add hot water half way up custard cups. Bake 45 minutes. Remove from oven, turn oven to broil. Add 1 t honey over each cup. Put under broiler for 5 minutes. Cool at least 4 hours in refrigerator.

Dirt Pudding
Anna Marie Schmucker

12 oz Oreo cookies
1 - 8 oz cream cheese
1 Lg box instant vanilla pudding
3 c milk

1 stick oleo or butter
1 c powdered sugar
1 - 12 oz Cool Whip

Crush cookies. Put 3/4 of them in a 9x13 inch pan. Cream together the oleo and cream cheese. Mix in powdered sugar and add Cool Whip, set aside. Mix pudding with 3 c milk. Mix together with cream cheese mixture. Pour over cookie crumbs and sprinkle rest of Oreo crumbs on top. Chill 2 hours.

Banana Pie
Theme Buffet: Fiddler on the Roof - *Chef Brenda Ritter*

1 1/4 oz gelatin
1 c boiling water
1 ripe banana
2 Tbsp lemon juice

1/2 c sugar
12 oz cream cheese - soft
1/2 c sour cream
1 tsp vanilla

Combine gelatin and sugar, add water and set aside. Beat cream and cheese until fluffy. Add mashed banana. Beat until blended. Add gelatin mix. Beat again, add sour cream, lemon juice, and vanilla. Beat until very smooth. Chill several hours or over night.

Frozen Peaches
Laura Slabaugh

17 to 20 lbs peaches before peeled (1/2 bushel)
7 c sugar
8 oz frozen orange juice (mix with water)

Mix sugar and juice well before. Pour over sliced peaches. Freeze

French Chocolate Roll

Theme Buffet: **Fiddler on the Roof -** *Chef Brenda Ritter*

6 oz semi-sweet chocolate
1 tsp vanilla extract
1/8 tsp salt
3 Tbsp powdered sugar divided
3 Tbsp unsweetened cocoa powder divided
1 c diced maraschino cherries

2 Tbsp strong coffee
6 eggs, separated
3/4 c sugar
1 c heavy cream

Preheat oven to 350 degrees. Grease 15x10x1 inch jelly roll pan; line with wax paper, extending it a few inches from the narrow ends. Melt chocolate in coffee over low heat. Remove from heat; stir in vanilla until smooth and set aside to cool. In a large bowl, beat egg whites with salt until soft peaks form. Add sugar, one tablespoon at a time beating well until mixture forms stiff shining peaks; set aside. Stir egg yolks to break up. Stir chocolate mixture into egg yolks until well blended. Fold 1/4 of egg white mixture into chocolate mixture until well blended. Add to remaining egg whites; fold gently until blended. Pour into prepared pan and spread evenly. Bake 16 to 18 minutes or until top is firm. Remove from oven; run small knife around the edges to loosen cake. Sift 2 tablespoons each of cocoa and powdered sugar onto clean towel. Invert pan onto coated towel. Working quickly, remove pan and peel wax paper; cool completely. Beat cream with remaining 1 tablespoon cocoa and powdered sugar until stiff. Spread over cake to within 1/2 inch of edges. Lift one side of towel until cake rolls inward; continue until cake is rolled. Roll will have cracks. Trim off edges.

Fruit Magic Cobbler

Kathy Hockert

1 can Cherry pie filling
1/4 c Butter - melted

1 pkg White cake mix (Jiffy)

Spread pie filling in 8 x 8 square pan. Combine mix in bowl with soft butter and mix till crumbly. Sprinkle over top of pie filling. Bake at 350 for 45 minutes.

Frozen Ice Cream Dessert
Frieda Miller

2 1/2 c cream filled chocolate cookie crumbs, divided
1/2 gallon chocolate or vanilla ice cream, softened
1/2 c butter, melted   1/2 c white sugar
1 1/2 c salted peanuts, optional   1 - 8 oz Cool Whip

Chocolate Sauce:
2 c powdered sugar   1/2 c butter, melted
2/3 c semisweet chocolate chips 1 tsp vanilla
1 - 12 oz can evaporated milk

Combine 2 cups cookie crumbs with butter and sugar. Press into bottom of a 9x13x2 inch pan. Freeze for 15 minutes. Spread ice cream over crumbs; freeze until firm, about 3 hours. Meanwhile; combine first four sauce ingredients in a sauce pan; bring to a boil. Boil for 8 minutes. Remove from heat and stir in vanilla; allow to cool to room temperature. Spoon sauce over ice cream; sprinkle with nuts. Freeze until firm. Spread cool whip over nuts and sprinkle with remaining cookie crumbs. Freeze at least 3 hours before serving. Can be stored in freezer for up to a week.

Frozen Pumpkin Parfait
Nancy Hershberger

1 1/2 c graham cracker crumbs   1/4 c sugar
1/4 c melted butter   1 1/2 c pumpkin
1/2 c brown sugar   1/2 tsp salt
1/8 tsp cloves   1/4 tsp ginger

Mix graham cracker crumbs, sugar and butter and press into bottom of 9 inch square pan. Combine rest of ingredients in bowl. Fold in 1 quart softened vanilla ice cream. Pour on top of crumb base. Cover and place in freezer until firm. Top with chopped pecans and whipped cream (optional).

Frozen Strawberry Dessert
Audrie Yoder-Fuchs

1 can strawberry pie mix
1 can crushed pineapple (drained)
2 c miniature marshmallows

1 - 9 oz Cool Whip
1 can Eagle brand milk

Mix together and freeze.

Homemade Ice Cream
Amish Acres Kitchen

9 eggs
1 1/2 tsp salt
3 cans milnot or 1 qt half & half

7 1/2 c sugar
6 tsp vanilla
1 1/2 gal milk

Beat eggs well. Add sugar, salt, vanilla beat well. Add milnot and milk. Freeze

Orange Pudding
Velda Kuhns, great-great granddaughter of M.T. Kuhns

2 small boxes orange Jell-O
8 oz cream cheese
2 c Rich's Topping, whipped

3 c boiling water
1 c sugar
Mandarin oranges

Mix Jell-O well in boiling water; cool but don't let set. Cream cream cheese, add sugar and topping. Beat in Jell-O mixture with beater. Let set 3 hours or more. Put mandarin oranges on top.

Lady Bradford's Banana & Ginger Steamed Pudding
Theme Buffet: My Fair Lady - *Chef Brenda Ritter*

4 oz butter
1 tsp baking soda
2 eggs
1 c fresh whole wheat bread crumbs
2 pieces caramelized ginger, crumbled

8 Tbsp dark brown sugar
1 mashed banana
1/4 tsp salt

Cream butter and sugar, blend in banana and ginger. Dissolve baking soda in a little warm water. Add bread crumbs, eggs, salt and baking soda to banana mixture, mix well. Place all in well greased 5 cup pudding bowl. Cover with foil pleated down the middle, fasten it around the rim of the bowl with a rubber band & place in large sauce pan in 3 inches of water on a steamer rack. Cover and steam for 2 hours, checking from time to time, making sure water is not evaporated. Add more water as needed. To serve and remove bowl from pan, run a knife gently around edge of bowl. Turn the pudding onto a serving dish. Serve hot.

Lemon Dessert
Kathy Hockert

1 c flour
8 oz cream cheese
1 c Cool Whip
2 - 3 oz lemon instant pudding mix

1/2 c oleo
1 c powdered sugar
3 c milk

Mix flour and oleo, bake in 350 degree oven until brown. Cool. Mix cream cheese, powdered sugar, cool whip. Put over flour and oleo when cooled. Mix lemon pudding mix and milk to make pudding. Pour on top of cream cheese mixture. Put Cool Whip on top.

Linzer Torte
Theme Buffet: The Sound of Music - *Chef Brenda Ritter*

1 c butter	1/2 c sugar
2 large egg yolks	2 1/2 c flour
10 oz seedless raspberry preserves	4 egg whites
2 c almond or walnuts, finely ground	1 c sugar (to combine with nuts)

In bowl, beat butter and 1/2 c sugar until light and fluffy. Add egg yolks and beat until well blended. Add flour and work with hands kneading until smooth. Press into 12x7 inch jelly roll pan. Bake 15 to20 minutes at 350 degrees until lightly browned. Remove from oven and spread with raspberry preserves and set aside. Beat egg whites until stiff. Combine cup of sugar and nuts and fold into egg whites. Spread over cake. Put cake back in oven for 25 minutes. Cool slightly but cut while still very warm. Cut into squares and cool.

Peach Tapioca
Laura Slabaugh

2 c boiling water	1 c sugar
2 c sliced peaches	5 Tbsp tapioca
Pinch of salt	1 tsp vanilla
10 large marshmallows	

Combine boiling water, sugar, peaches and tapioca. Cook for 5 minutes then add a pinch of salt, vanilla, and marshmallows. Stir well and refrigerate

Oreo Dessert
Ruth Ann Miller

Make 2 days ahead

Crust
20 crushed Oreos
Filling

1 1/2 large Cool Whip	2 c miniature marshmallows
1 1/4 c crushed dinner mints	

Top
8 Oreos

© Amish Acres, Nappanee, Indiana

Peach Bavarian
Bertha Hershberger

1 - 16 oz can sliced peaches
2 - 3 oz pkgs peach or apricot Jell-O
1 tsp almond extract
Additional sliced peaches

1/2 c sugar
2 c boiling water
8 oz whipped topping

Drain peaches and reserve 2/3 c juice. Chop peaches, set aside. In a bowl dissolve Jell-O and sugar in water. Stir in reserved peach juice. Chill until slightly thickened. Stir extract into whipped topping and gently fold into gelatin mixture. Fold in peaches. Pour into greased 6 cup mold. Chill overnight. Unfold, garnish with additional peaches

Pineapple Cake and Topping
Mrs. Paul Kuhns, great-grandson of M.T. Kuhns

1 box yellow cake mix
1 c pineapple juice from drained pineapple

2 eggs

Topping:
1 c milk
Whipped topping
Coconut
1 - 3.4 oz pkg instant vanilla pudding

1 - 8 oz cream cheese, softened
Crushed pineapple
Chopped nuts

Mix yellow cake mix, eggs and pineapple juice. Bake in 9x13 inch pan for 35 to 40 minutes at 350 degrees. Cool. Mix milk, cream cheese until smooth. Add rest of ingredients. Spread on cooled cake. Refrigerate any remaining.

Plum Pudding
Theme Buffet: Hello, Dolly! - *Chef Brenda Ritter*

1 lb suet, ground
1 1/2 lb sugar
2 Tbsp flour
1 lb raisins
1 Tbsp salt

1 lb bread crumbs
6 eggs, beaten
1 lb currants
1 Tbsp nutmeg

Mix all together and steam for 4 hours. Cover pan with wax paper while steaming.

Sauce:
1 c sugar, brown or white
2 c boiling water
1 Tbsp vanilla
Cold water

2 Tbsp butter
1 Tbsp vinegar
2 Tbsp cornstarch

Bring sugar and hot water, vinegar and cornstarch with cold water together and cook until thick. Add butter and vanilla, beat with spoon until smooth.

Rhubarb Cobbler
Brenda Beehler

3 c rhubarb
3 Tbsp flour

1 c sugar
1 tsp cinnamon

Topping:
1 c brown sugar
1 c oatmeal

1 c flour
1/2 c butter

Combine ingredients, pour into greased 9x9 inch pan. Mix topping ingredients together and crumble over top. Bake at 375 degrees for 40 minutes.

Rhubarb Delight
Mrs. Paul Hochstetler

1 c flour
1/2 tsp salt
1 egg, beaten
2 c rhubarb
1/2 c flour
1/4 c melted butter

1 tsp baking powder
2 Tbsp margarine
2 Tbsp milk
1 - 3 oz strawberry Jell-O
1 c sugar

Sift together flour, baking powder and salt. Cut in margarine. Stir in egg and milk. Pat in bottom of pan. Cover with rhubarb. Sprinkle with Jell-O. Top with flour, sugar and melted butter mixture. Bake at 350 degrees until golden brown.

Rizolago: Rice Pudding
Theme Buffet: Zorba - *Chef Brenda Ritter*

1/2 c rice
1/2 tsp cinnamon
1/2 tsp salt

1 qt milk
1/2 c sugar

Pour into greased custard cups. Bake at 275 degrees for 3 hours. Stir frequently for 1st hour. Add 1 Tbsp raisins during last 1/2 hour. Sprinkle with mixture of sugar & cinnamon.

Tortes
Theme Buffet: Smoke on the Mountain - *Chef Brenda Ritter*

1 1/2 c sugar and 1 1/2 c shortening creamed together
12 eggs
3 tsp vanilla
1 Tbsp baking powder
3/4 cup sugar

9 Tbsp milk
3 c cake flour
3/4 tsp salt

Mix milk and vanilla with (12) eggs yolks one at a time. Add cream mixture. Mix in cake flour, baking powder and salt, until smooth. In separate bowl beat egg whites with a pinch of salt until peaks form. Add sugar one tablespoon at a time until glossy. Spread over cakes. Bake for 30 minutes.

Strawberry Pretzel Dessert
Laura Slabaugh

3/4 c margarine
2 1/2 c crushed pretzels (not too fine)
1 c sugar (scant)
1 - 6 oz strawberry Jell-O
3 c chilled strawberries

3 Tbsp brown sugar
1 - 8 oz cream cheese
1 small carton Cool Whip
2 c boiling water

Cream margarine and brown sugar. Mix with crushed pretzels.
Pat into buttered pan and bake 10 minutes at 350 degrees. Cream
the cream cheese and sugar. Fold in Cool Whip and spread over
cooled crust. Dissolve Jell-O in boiling water and let cool. When
Jell-O mixture begins to set add strawberries and pour over cream
cheese mixture. You may garnish with Cool Whip.
Instead of the Jell-O mixture I take 2 packs of strawberry danish
dessert and cook according to pie filling directions then I add a
quart of frozen whole strawberries and it cools enough to add to
cream cheese mixture. It's better - plus quicker.

Tapioca Pudding
Amish Acres Kitchen

1 - 2 lb can pineapple drained (save juice)
1 large can mandarin oranges (halved, drained, save juice)
6 c liquid (including syrup drained from fruit and water)
1/2 c baby pearl tapioca
1 c sugar
1 - 8 oz container of frozen whipped topping, thawed
   or 1 pint heavy cream, whipped and sweetened to taste

1 - 3 oz pkg orange gelatin
1 pinch of salt

Drain fruit and set aside. Add water to fruit syrup to make 6 cups
of liquid. Bring to boil and add tapioca. Boil 15 minutes. Let stand
10 minutes. Add gelatin, sugar and salt. When mixture is cool, stir
in pineapple and oranges. Let stand in refrigerator. Just before serving, stir in whipped topping or whipping cream.

Turtles
Susan Nunemaker

Caramel:

1 c milk
1 c white Karo syrup
1 pinch of salt

1 box light brown sugar
1/2 lb butter
1 tsp vanilla

Cook till soft ball. Take 1 pound pecans & place in 3's on foil to resemble a turtle shape.

Chocolate:

2 large Hershey bars

1/6 bar of parafin wax

Melt Hershey bars with 1/6 stick of parafin wax (depending on size). Pour the above caramel mixture on pecans by spoon. Then do the same with chocolate mixture. Let cool.

Upside Down Date Pudding
Dorcas Mishler, great-granddaughter of M.T. Kuhns

1 c cut of dates
1/2 c brown sugar
1 egg
1 1/3 c flour
1/2 tsp baking powder
1 c chopped nuts

1 c boiling water
1/2 c white sugar
2 Tbsp melted butter
1 tsp soda
1/2 tsp salt

Combine dates and boiling water. Let set until cool. Cream sugars, egg and butter until light. Add flour and rest of ingredients, stir in nuts and cooled date mixture. Mix well. Combine 1 1/2 c brown sugar, 2 t butter and 1 1/2 c boiling water. Pour this in your cake pan first, then top with mixture. Bake at 375 degrees for 40 to 45 minutes.

Miscellaneous

Bon Bon Candy
Ruth Ann Miller

1 1/2 lb powdered sugar
1 c Eagle Brand milk
1 package angel flake coconut

1/2 c butter, softened
1 c nuts, chopped
Vanilla

Mix ingredients and chill. Form into balls. Chill overnight. Melt 1 large pkg Chocolate Chips (12 oz) and 1 block or square paraffin. Dip balls while hot.

Brown Sugar Grapenuts
Marlene Hershberger, great-grandson of M.T. Kuhns

4 c brown sugar
4 tsp soda
1 tsp maple flavor
1 tsp salt

2 qt buttermilk or sour milk
5 lbs graham flour
1 tsp vanilla

Mix all together then bake as a cake at 350 degrees. Let cool then crumble up & dry in warm oven. Makes a good breakfast cereal.

Caramel Corn
Susan Nunemaker

1 c white sugar
1 c dark corn syrup
1/2 tsp soda

1 c brown sugar
1/4 lb butter

Cook until the syrup spins a thread. Add soda. When the soda puffs the syrup up, pour in to popcorn. Stir until all the popcorn separates.

Caramels
Ruth Ann Miller

2 c sugar
1/4 lb butter
1 tsp vanilla

3/4 c syrup
1 pt cream

Combine syrup, sugar, butter and half of cream, cook until boiling. Add other half of cream. Stir constantly. Cook until 220 degrees. Add vanilla pour into pan. Cool. Cut.

Cinnamon Popcorn
Laura Slabaugh

8 qts plain popped corn
1/2 c light corn syrup

1 c butter or oleo
1 - 9 oz pkg red hot candy

Place popcorn in a large bowl and set aside. In a sauce pan combine butter, corn syrup and candies, bring to a boil over medium heat, stirring constantly. Boil for 5 minutes stirring occasionally. Pour over popcorn and mix thoroughly. Turn into 2 greased 15x10 inch baking pans. Bake at 250 degrees for 1 hour stirring every 15 minutes. Remove from pans onto waxed paper to cool. Break apart and store in air tight container.

Elephant Ears
Sherry Maurer

3 egg yolks
6 Tbsp cold water
2 c flour
Powered sugar or cinnamon/sugar mix

1 whole egg
1 tsp salt
2 or 3 inches of oil

Beat yolks and egg for 8 minutes. Add water and salt.
Work in flour until dough is soft, but not sticky. Add more water, if necessary. Divide dough into 8 equal pieces and flatten each into a circle. Deep fry and sprinkle with powdered sugar or cinnamon/sugar mixture.

187

Fondue Marinade
Ruby Fry, granddaughter of M.T. Kuhns

1/2 medium onion, chopped   1 c Wesson oil
1/2 c soy sauce

Mix ingredients in blender or shaker. Pour over meat & marinate 12 to 24 hours. Grill meat.

Giblet Gravy
Amish Acres Thresher Dinner

1 bag turkey giblets (gizzard, liver)   1 qt water
1 Tbsp Lawry seasoned salt   1/2 tsp celery salt
1/2 tsp garlic salt   2 Tbsp salad oil
1 to 1 1/2 c flour   1/4 tsp yellow food coloring
Dash of Kitchen Bouquet

Boil giblets in seasoned water. Remove giblets from broth, cut into bits. Make gravy, stir enough flour to make a smooth paste. Stir coloring and bouquet into hot broth. Stir until thick and smooth. Add cut up giblets.

Hidden Valley Ranch Dressing
Mrs. Freeman Mishler, great-grandchild of M.T. Kuhns

2 c mayonnaise   1 tsp parsley flakes
1/2 tsp onion flakes   1/2 Tbsp garlic salt
1/2 tsp celery salt   2 c buttermilk or sour cream

Mix all ingredients and shake. Do not blend.
For dip use only 1 cup buttermilk.

Horseradish Sauce
Theme Buffet: Smoke on the Mountain - Chef Brenda Ritter

1 c horseradish   1/2 c heavy cream

Whip cream until firm, mix in horseradish.

Homemade Yogurt
Mary Kuhns, granddaughter of M.T. Kuhns

1 qt skim milk

2 Tbsp yogurt

(Your first time - use store bought plain yogurt)
Heat milk to just below boiling point. Pour it in a glass jar. Cool it so you can stand your hand against the jar. Add plain yogurt and mix well. Set the jar in water same temperature as the milk. Set in a warm place, such as in the oven over the pilot light etc. to keep it warm. After it has thickened remove jar from water. Let cool & refrigerate. Enjoy. Save 2 Tablespoon for your next batch each time.

Ketchup
Ervin Bontrager Jr., great-grandson of M.T. Kuhns

2 gallons tomatoes
2 large onions
9 heaping Tbls Clear-Jel
1/2 tsp cinnamon
8 - 6 oz cans tomato paste

2 c vinegar
6 c brown sugar
1/2 tsp cloves
6 Tbsp salt

Boil first 3 ingredients & boil till onions are soft, put through Victoria Strainer. Put back to boil. Mix clear-jel, cloves, & cinnamon with water and add tomatoes, boil 10 minutes. Add tomato paste, helps thicken it and gives a nice red color. Can & enjoy. Makes around 12 quarts.

Marshmallow Fluff Frosting
Mrs. Melvin Kuhns, great-grandson of M.T. Kuhns

1/3 c egg whites
1/2 c sugar
1/2 tsp cream of tarter
1 tsp vanilla

3/4 c Karo syrup, light
1/4 tsp salt
4 to 6 large marshmallows

Put first 5 ingredients into the top of a large double boiler. Beat constantly with a beater until the icing becomes white and rather thick. Add the marshmallows and vanilla, continue beating until melted and contents are thick.

Muleteer's Ears
Theme Buffet: Man of La Mancha - *Chef Brenda Ritter*

1 1/2 c milk	1 c sugar
2 Tbsp sugar	1 1/2 tsp salt
6 Tbsp vegetable shortening	2 packages active dry yeast
4 c flour	2 tsp cinnamon

In saucepan combine sugar, salt and shortening. Bring to boil, cool to lukewarm. Add yeast, whisk until dissolved. Add 2 cups flour at a time. Beat until smooth after each addition. Pour in greased bowl and let rise 45 minutes. Pat out in ear shape. Deep fry at 375 degrees until brown.

Party Mix
Ruth Kuhns, great-granddaughter of M.T. Kuhns

1 box Chex cereal	2 c mixed nuts
1 box Chicken in a Biscuit crackers	1 bag pretzels
1 box Ritz Bits	1 box Bugles
1 box Better Cheddar crackers	

Put all in a large garbage bag. Add 2 small packages Hidden Valley Ranch mix and 1 cup canola oil. Shake to mix. Put in containers, but do not seal tightly for 12 hours.

Peanut Log
Jacob and Loretta Kuhns, great-grandson of M.T. Kuhns

1 c sugar	1 c Karo corn syrup
1 c peanut butter	3 c Rice Krispies
3 c Cheerios	1 1/2 c dry roasted peanuts

Melt first 3 ingredients together, then pour over rest of ingredients. Put in cake pan. Cool. Cut in bars.

Perfect Sausage Gravy
Andrea Stahly

1 lb sausage	4 Tbsp flour
1 qt milk	Salt & Pepper

Brown meat, pour off grease. Add flour and brown lightly. Add milk and stir until smooth. Bring to a boil and add milk until desired consistency. Add salt and pepper to taste.

Pizza Dip
Lloyd Kuhns, great-grandson of M.T. Kuhns

1 - 8 oz cream cheese	1/2 c sour cream
1/8 tsp garlic powder	1 tsp oregano
1/8 tsp black pepper	1/2 c pizza sauce
1/2 c chopped onion	1/2 c chopped pepperoni
1/2 c chopped green pepper	

Mix together the first 5 ingredients in a 9x5 inch pan. Layer the 4 last ingredients on top. Bake at 350 degrees for 10 minutes. Add 1/2 c mozzarella cheese on top and bake 5 minutes longer. Mushrooms and black olives may be added. Serve warm with corn or tortilla chips.

Pizza Hut Sauce
Jacob and Loretta Kuhns, great-grandson of M.T. Kuhns

1/2 bushel tomatoes	3 to 4 medium onions
A bit of parsley	1 c sugar
1/2 c salt	1 tsp paprika
1 tsp red pepper	1 Tbsp chili powder
2 Tbsp garlic salt	2 Tbsp oregano
2 c Clear-jel mixed with a little water	

Cook first 3 ingredients together & run through sieve. To 3 gallons, add rest of ingredients & add to juice. Boil well. Cold pack 15 minutes.

Quick & Easy Fudge
Ruth Ann Miller

3 c sugar
2/3 c evaporated milk
1 - 7 oz marshmallow crème
1 package butter brickle bits

3/4 c oleo
2 c butterscotch chips
1 c pecans, chopped

Combine sugar, oleo and milk in pan. Bring to rolling boil stirring constantly for 5 minutes. Remove from heat. Stir in butterscotch chips till melted. Add marshmallow crème, nuts, butter brickle and vanilla. Beat with fork until well blended. Pour into greased 9x13 inch pan. Cool. Cut into squares.

Quince Marmalade
Amish Acres Kitchen

Wipe quinces, remove blossom ends, cut in quarters, remove seeds; then cut in small pieces. Put into a preserving kettle, and add enough water to nearly cover. Cook slowly until soft. Rub through a hair sieve, and add 3/4 its measure of heated sugar. Cook slowly 20 minutes, stirring to prevent burning. Put in tumblers.

Rhubarb Jam
Susan Nunemaker

6 c rhubarb
1 package Jell-O (strawberry)

4 c sugar
2 c water

Cut rhubarb very thin, mix sugar & rhubarb very well. Let stand overnight. Boil water, rhubarb and sugar mixture 20 minutes, add Jell-O, stir well till all is dissolved. Seal while hot. It will freeze.

Sandwich Spread
Mrs. Paul Hochstetler

3 large cucumbers   3 large onions
3 large carrots   3 large red peppers
3 large green peppers   1 bunch celery

Grind all but the celery, chop that up fine. Place 2 Tbsp salt on all
and let stand for a few hours. Drain dry. Add 1 1/2 pt vinegar, 2 c
white sugar, 4 Tbsp flour (rounded), 1 c prepared mustard. Pour
over vegetables. Cook 20 minutes, stirring constantly. Add 1/4 lb
butter. When cool add 1 pt salad dressing. Put in jars and seal.

Sausage Gravy
Mrs. Joseph Hostetler, Jr.

1 lb bulk pork sausage   1 qt milk
2 Tbsp finely chopped onions   6 Tbsp flour
1/2 tsp poultry seasoning   1/2 tsp ground nutmeg
1/4 tsp salt   Dash Worcestershire sauce
Angel biscuits

Crumble sausage into a large saucepan; cook over medium-low
heat. Add onions; cook and stir until transparent. Drain, discard-
ing all but 2 Tbsp of drippings. Stir in flour; cook over medium
heat about 6 minutes or until mixture bubbles & turns golden. Stir
in milk. Add seasonings; cook stirring, until thickened. To serve,
slice biscuits and spoon gravy over halves.

Scotch Eggs
Theme Buffet: Brigadoon - Chef Brenda Ritter

6 hard boiled eggs   1 lb sausage meat
Seasoned bread crumbs

Cover each egg completely with sausage meat. Roll in crumbs
to cover, cook in hot oil until bread crumbs are browned.
Turn frequently to cook evenly. Drain and cool. Slice to serve.

Sesame Dressing
Theme Buffet: Smoke on the Mountain - Chef Brenda Ritter

1 1/2 c sugar
2 tsp salt
3 Tbsp pureed onion
3 Tbsp toasted sesame seeds

2 tsp dry mustard
2/3 c white vinegar
2 c salad oil
2 tsp soy sauce

In food processor, mix sugar, mustard salt, vinegar, and soy sauce. Add onion juice and blend. Add oil slowly while processor is running and mix until thick. Add sesame seeds. Store in refrigerator.

Soft Pretzels
Bertha Hershberger

1 1/2 tsp yeast
1 1/2 tsp sugar
1 3/4 - 2 c flour

3/4 c warm water
1/2 tsp salt
1 egg

Mix and dissolve yeast, warm water, sugar, and salt. Stir in flour until it forms into a ball. Put dough on lightly floured surface and knead until smooth. Roll dough into small ropes and shape into pretzels. Place on greased cookie sheet. Beat an egg and brush on pretzels (unbaked). Sprinkle with coarse salt. Bake at 425 degrees for 12 to 15 minutes. Serve with warm cheese sauce.

Taffy
Ruth Ann Miller

2 c granulated sugar
1/2 c Karo syrup, white
1 tsp vanilla

1 c brown sugar
2 Tbsp butter
1 c water

Boil all ingredients, except to add vanilla. Pour into buttered platter until cool enough to handle. Then pull until white. Stretch out on table. Cut in 1 inch pieces with scissors - use butter or corn starch on hands when it gets sticky.

Spaghetti Sauce
Gloria Fimbianti

2 Tbsp butter	2 tsp vegetable oil
2 lbs ground meat (1/2 beef, 1/2 pork)	1 medium onion, chopped
1 large can tomato puree	1 small can tomato paste

Spices: sage rosemary, salt, pepper or Italian seasoning
Melt butter and oil in fry-pan. Sauté onion until soft (not brown). Add ground meat. Brown. Put mixture in sauce pan, add puree and paste. Add water and bouillon cube to drippings in fry-pan. Allow to boil. Then add to sauce pan. Paste should be diluted in small amount of water before adding to sauce pan. Add seasonings. Cook 3 hours on simmer. Stir frequently. Add spices in cheese cloth or tea ball so they are not loose in sauce. For garlic flavor a clove may be sautéed in the butter-oil combo before you add the chopped onion. Remove garlic before adding onion. The sauce should be cooked on low heat so it does not stick. Sprinkle ground cinnamon in sauce for flavor.

Twice Cooked Divinity
Nancy Hamman

3 c sugar	1 c light corn syrup
1/2 c water	1 c sugar
1/4 c water	3 egg whites
1 tsp vanilla	

Pan #1: Combine 3 c sugar, 1 c light corn syrup, 1/2 c water. Bring to hard ball. **Pan # 2:** Combine 1 c sugar, 1/4 c water. Boil to thread. In a large glass bowl beat 3 egg whites to stiff. Add and beat pan # 2 to egg whites. When #1 is hard ball add to above mix and add 1 tsp vanilla and color. Drop by spoon onto waxed paper.

Vanilla Caramels
Laura Slabaugh

1 1/2 c sugar
1/4 c butter
1/3 tsp salt

1 c light karo syrup
1 c cream
1 tsp vanilla

Combine all ingredients except vanilla. Place over low heat and cook to soft ball stage. Remove from heat and add vanilla. Pour in buttered pan. (Heat slowly till it boils then boil fast - this keeps them light.) You can also add chopped pecans. Wrap separately in waxed paper.

Marinated Potato Salad
Angie Pletcher-Stillson

3/4 lb whole new potatoes
3/4 c oil & vinegar dressing
1 can artichoke hearts, drained and halved
1 small green pepper, cut into strips
6 cherry tomatoes, halved
1/2 of a small red onion, separated into rings
1/4 c snipped parsley

Cook potatoes in boiling water for 15 minutes; drain well. Quarter potatoes. In a large bowl pour dressing over potatoes. Add artichoke hearts, green pepper, tomatoes and onion. Chill for 4 to 24 hours, stirring occasionally. Transfer to a serving bowl. Garnish with parsley and a kale leaf, if desired. Makes 5 side dish servings.

Notes

Nappanee, Indiana

The award winning restaurant, hotels, theatre,
shops and tours have earned Amish Acres
in Nappanee, Indiana, the designation
of "Indiana's number-one tourist attraction"
by *Travel Trade Magazine*.

Documentary Films
& House and Farm Tour

Your visit to Amish Acres begins with two documentary films; *Genesis* and *Exodus*. The films are shown in the Locke Township Meeting House in the Greeting Barn immediately before the house & farm tour.

The House and Farm Tour is a 45-minute guided walking tour of the Stahly-Nissley-Kuhns farmstead tracing the history of the pioneering Amish families of northern Indiana. Tours depart every 30 minutes starting on the hour at the sound of the dinner bell from the Buggy Shed. It's an easy walk at a leisurely pace.

Horse Drawn Buggy Ride

Open black buggies and sleek driving horses trot along split rail fences on gravel lanes into Amish Acres woods and lend a nostalgic moment to your visit. The 15-minute pleasure ride departs on a first come basis from the Buggy Shed.

Countryside Tour

Hop aboard Amish Acres passenger van where an experienced local guide narrates while you enjoy the sights and sounds of area Amish farms clustered along the backroads of Nappanee. You'll travel along some of Nappanee's most scenic country roads past Amish homes and fields.

Craft Demonstrations

Amish Acres demonstrations are seasonal and vary by the day - much like the daily chores of a working Amish farm. Please call ahead for tour schedules, hours and demonstrations. On the farm, crafts and chores still follow the flow of the seasons. Maple syrup, apple butter, sorghum molasses and dried foods are produced here just as they were hundreds of years ago. You'll see how Amish quilts are created, watch demonstrations of lye soap and broom making and experience the art of rug weaving.

Historic Outbuildings

Amish Acres is home to many authentic historic buildings which have been relocated, refurbished and now surround the farm's pond. As you walk the grounds at your own pace you'll view among many others the ice house, saw mill, mint still, one-room school house and Chauncy Thomas Blacksmith Shop. Relax on benches and watch the various waterfowl that frequent the pond.

Restaurant Barn

The century-old Restaurant Barn features oaken floorboards, oilcloth covered tables and hand-hewn beams that set the proper mood for the award-winning family style Threshers Dinner. The Barn Loft Grill serves lunch featuring soup, sandwiches, salads and onion rings.

The Cow Shed

Enter a place like no other. The Cow Shed sets itself apart from other craft shops with its unique displays and whimsical cow theme. The Cow Shed is filled to the rafters with Amish-made goods, hand-stitched quilts and bulk food all displayed creatively throughout the shop.

The Greeting Barn

The Greeting Barn has two floors of gifts, crafts, antiques, baskets, quilts, souvenirs, accessories, and Amish country knickknacks to be explored. The gift shop includes unique products exclusive to Amish Acres - handmade Amish dolls each named and numbered are just a sample of what can be found. The children's corner is filled with stuffed animals, whimsical puzzles, candy sticks, books and Beanie Babies.

Soda Shop & Fudgery Cabin

The antique marble soda fountain offers up a variety of delicious treats from sodas, malts and ice cream to old fashioned fountain drinks and slices of homemade pie a la mode.

The Fudgery is filled with the aroma of handmade chocolates of every shape, flavor and size. Choose from chocolate covered cherries, peanuts, almonds and pretzels, chewy turtles, and soft meltaways. Take home as much homemade fudge as you wish and watch the candies actually being made right behind the counter.

W.H. Best & Sons Meat & Cheese Shop

This log cabin stocks some of the most flavorful and numerous varieties of meats and cheeses to be found. Enjoy giant dill pickles and a variety of cool drinks.

The Bakery

The bakery bakes fresh daily for the restaurant as well as the counter and shelf. Take home a dozen molasses or chocolate chip cookies, a bag of egg noodles, as well as loaves of our famous hearth bread, stollen bread, strudels, fruit pies and of course our award-winning Shoofly pie. (*The Chicago Tribune* declares it "The Best!")

The School Belfry

The School Belfry features original works from across the country by over 200 invited artists and crafters from the award winning Amish Acres Arts & Crafts Festival.

Indiana's Only Resident Musical Repertory Theatre Company

The National Home of *Plain & Fancy*

an Amish Acres tradition, since 1986, *Plain & Fancy* fills the proscenium Joseph Stein Stage each April through November. This gentle but spirited musical comedy brought the first national attention to the quaint customs, stern morals and picturesque dress of the Amish. Over 2,500 shows have now been performed, and over 225,000 patrons have marveled at Amish Acres nationally recruited cast, English Strand theatre lighting, full-scale, authentic sets and costumes over the last decade.

Amish Acres proudly presents *Plain & Fancy* in rotating repertory with five additional Broadway musicals throughout the nine month theatre season. You can even see three different plays in two days on Amish Acres Round Barn Theatre stage!

The stage is proudly dedicated to Joseph Stein, author of Plain & Fancy, Fiddler on the Roof *and* Zorba.

"Of all the regional theatres with which I have worked, The Round Barn Theatre is my favorite."

-Joseph Stein

Historic Farm, Restaurants, Theatre, Shops & Inns

Award Winning
Threshers Dinner

A typical menu, it's all on the table.

Iron kettle of thick ham & bean soup
Amish Acres freshly baked hearth bread
Fresh yellow butter
Crock of locally made apple butter

Seasonal relish
Sweet & sour cabbage salad

Green beans with smoked side meat
Beef & noodles
Mashed potatoes
Sage dressing & giblet gravy

Festive roast turkey
Broasted country chicken
Cider-baked hickory smoked ham
Tender roast beef

Fresh fruit pies
Shoo-fly pie
Vanilla date nut pudding

Coffee
Hot tea
Milk
Lemonade
Iced tea